I0024686

Naomi Katz

# Beautiful

Being an Empowered
Young Woman

**Newly Revised and Updated**

To my mom,

and my grandmothers before her
for illuminating my path from the stars

and to Byron Preiss

and the eternal dance of love
between fathers and daughters

i

iBooks

Habent Sua Fata Libelli

Manhanset House
Dering Harbor, New York 11965
Tel: 212-427-7139
bricktower@aol.com | www.ibooksinc.com

All rights reserved under the International and Pan-
American Copyright Conventions. Printed in the United
States by J. Boylston & Company, Publishers, New York.
No part of this publication may be reproduced, stored
in a retrieval system, or transmitted in any form or
by any means, electronic, or otherwise, without the
prior written permission of the copyright holder.
The ibooks colophon is a trademark of J. Boylston
& Company, Publishers.

Library of Congress Cataloging-in-Publication Data
**Beautiful—Being an Empowered Young Woman** (2nd Ed.)
Katz, Naomi p. cm.

1. Psychology: Developmental—Adolescent
2. Psychology: Psychotherapy—Child & Adolescent
3. Family & Relationships: Life Stages—Teenagers
Non-Fiction, I. Title.

978-1-59687-860-0 Trade Paper
Copyright © 2016 by Naomi Katz
July 2019

**Design** | Keren and Golan Studio—
Keren Gafni and Nitsan Lear
**Illustration** | Danielle Peleg
**Editing** | Lahevet Pollack

Second Trade Paper Edition
First Printing

# CONTENTS

## Preface

Writing *Beautiful* was a journey unto itself that began when the father of one of my former students asked me to create something to support his daughters, to feed his relationship with his girls. He knew about my work because his eldest daughter had been in my class when I started teaching in New York, over 20 years ago, at the school in which I facilitated my first girls' group. That group formed after girls at that school reached out to me, asking for support. I was only 21 then and in many ways still an adolescent myself. Though I was nervous, I responded to their request and together we embarked on an incredible journey, exploring what being a woman meant to each of us and how we could support one another as we discovered our own inner voices.

Years later, when I set out on the mission to manifest my book, I was working exclusively with girls, facilitating groups in a variety of contexts, with girls of a wide range of ages. The stories I share in this book are all true; this creation is a compilation of the experiences of a large and diverse group of girls coming of age in our time. These experiences are shared through the eyes of their mentor, a woman who herself was once a teen girl and who acutely remembers—as I imagine we all do—how it felt to transform from a girl into a woman. That girl, that woman, is me.

The second edition of *Beautiful* is the result of my experience working with the first edition. Since it was published in 2016, I have spoken with countless girls and adults (mostly parents and educators) who have read the book. I listened to them in order to learn what has helped them and where they needed more. These conversations led me to write a new chapter about social media and to revise a great deal more, particularly the chapter about sex and sexuality, in order to meet the needs of an increasingly confusing culture.

Somehow, in this age when life moves very fast and nearly everything is virtual, a book still has the power to give its readers a sense of inner quiet. This book allows readers the chance to stop, listen to our inner voices, and practice connecting to our true selves. In an era when growing into an adult is confusing, one of the greatest gifts we can give our youth is support as they cultivate their ability to listen to themselves and make decisions that nourish them.

To me, the most important feature of this book is its authenticity. I write about what I know, authentically, and I think this helps my readers FEEL my authentic voice and connect with their own. I speak directly about meanness because it happened to me. A lot. I share my own vulnerabilities about coming of age and understanding myself as a sexual being because that journey really shaped my adolescence. I don't write about what I don't know. I share my own perspectives about race as a white woman, and I asked my students to share theirs as women of color. I don't write about coming out because I didn't. I share my observations about teens and social media, and I also understand that the way young people are interacting with these technologies is different from the way I use them.

To the mothers and adult women who encounter this book: We are the elders of this time. We are the role models our girls admire. Each of us has wisdom to impart to the next generation. We need to collaborate—whether we are mothers or not—in our collective human journey, raising the next generation.

May every girl and every woman know that she always has someone to turn to, someone with whom she can celebrate her victories and cry her tears.

The father who dreamt this book into existence never held it in his hands. His life on earth came to an end very shortly before I finished writing. This book honors his legacy, the vision he carried for his daughters. And so, this book honors the special relationship between fathers and daughters. This book honors the harmony between men and women, the union that is the source of life. Equality for all rests on collaboration, mutual recognition and respect.

May every boy have the opportunity to reflect and understand what kind of man he wants to be and how he wants to relate to women. May the men teach the boys about masculinity, and may they together explore what it means to express it healthily.

My mother also did not live to see the birth of this book. Its message—that we deserve to be loved just as we are—is the legacy my mother left behind. Everyone felt loved in her presence. May we all be blessed to love ourselves with the care and passion with which my mother taught me to love myself, through the example of her love for me. I am the woman that I am because of her, because of my grandmothers. I do what I do because I carry their teachings, their love, inside of me. I am the continuation of their steps upon this earth.

This book honors the steps of all the women who have walked upon this earth, in all times. All of the experiences that have been lived, in all of the generations, that comprise what it means to be a woman.

Thank you to my students, who inspired this creation and continue to awaken me every day. To my dad and my sister, Aviva, and to my dear husband, Robert, who continually teaches me what it means for a man and a woman to live in love. To my maestra, Carmen Vicente, who always reminds me to direct my words and sow seeds of love in the hearts of others. To my grandmothers and my mother, dancing together in the stars, who taught me what it is to be a woman.

In gratitude to the generations of women who walked the earth before me, and the secrets they carried.

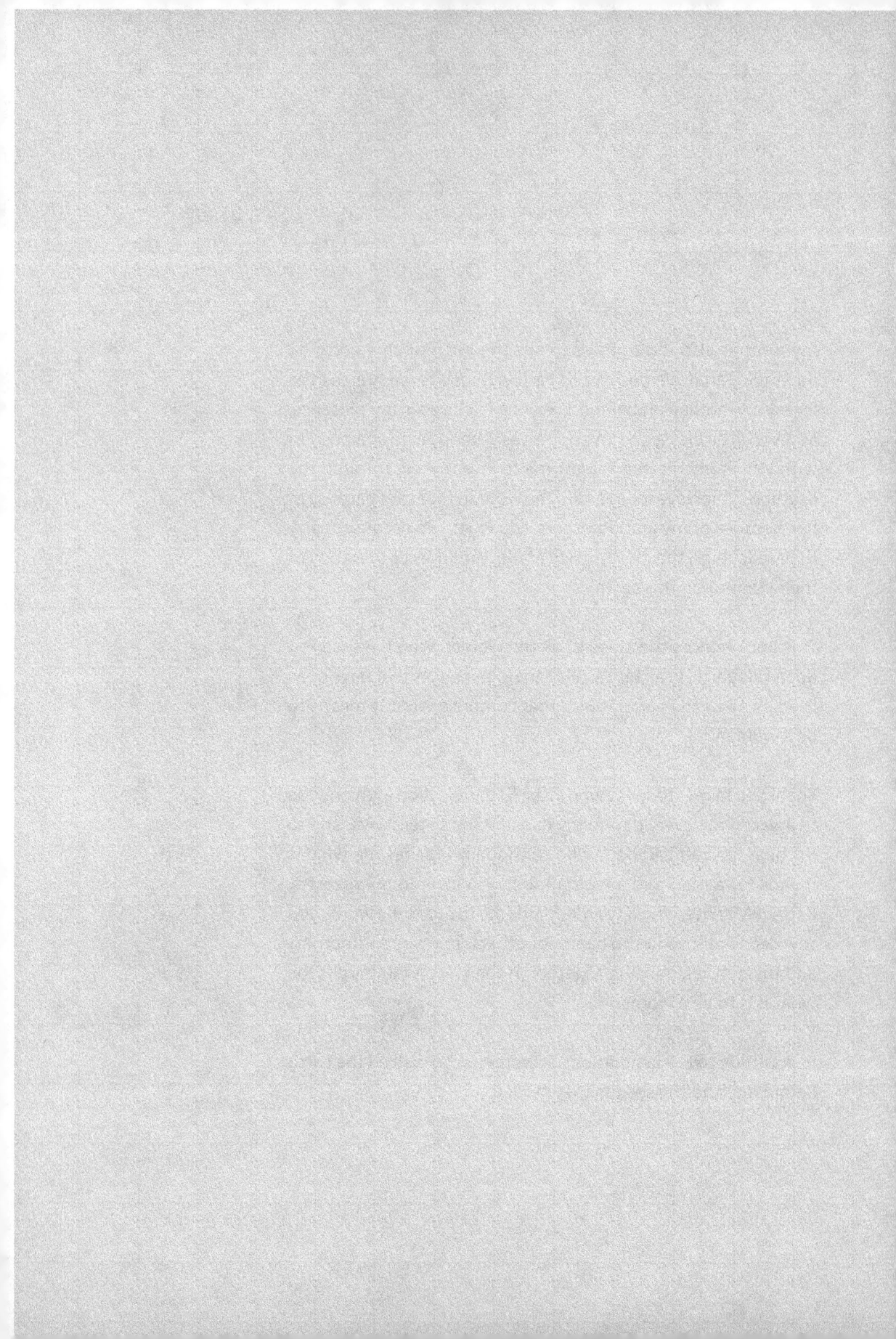

INTRODUCTION

# Why I Wrote This Book
# and Why You Might Want to Read It

"Hey baby! Lookin' good! Can I get your number?"
I turn on my heel. "Who the hell do you think you are? You think
you can talk to me like that? Yeah, I'll give you my number—
right after you kiss my feet, you jerk! I bet your mother wouldn't
be too proud of you talking like that to women on the street!
How would you feel if someone called your sister out like that?
Huh? HUH?!!!!"

Or at least that was the scene I imagined in my head. In the
real story, I simply looked straight ahead and kept walking. I
wanted to say something to this loser, I really did, but I kept
my mouth shut. I'm not sure why. I'm not a shy person, and I
definitely stand up for myself. Maybe I was scared he would
say something back to me, or even hurt me. I don't know. But
that scene replayed itself over a thousand times while I lived in
New York City. I can't count the number of times guys I'd never
met called me out on the street, as if this was a normal way
to talk to women. After a while, it really started to get to me. I
started to wonder, "Was this happening to other women too?"

## About those catcalls

I'm not sure if guys think they are going to win your affection by calling you out, but they must have a reason beyond simply harassing women. I can't imagine what that reason is, though, when they say things like:

*Nice ass!*

*Sweet rack!*

*What's your name, hot stuff?*

*Want to get in my car? (ALWAYS SAY NO!)*

*Ohhh, what I would do with you if I could...*

*Where's your boyfriend?*

The list goes on forever. But honestly, the worst of all is the guy who doesn't say anything. He just looks at you in that creepy way, and you know he is undressing you with his eyes. Just being looked at like that makes me feel like I need a shower.

## Feeling like a piece of meat?

I was a seventh-grade teacher while I was living in New York City, and many of my students were attractive young women who looked a lot more like college students than middle-school kids. Were they getting called out and leered at too?

Lara was in eighth grade. She was very tall and thin, and looked like a supermodel. We were very close, and I knew if I asked her a question, she'd answer me honestly.

"Lara, can I ask you something?"

"Sure, Katzie, what's up?"

"When you're walking around on the street, do random guys call you out and tell you things they want to do to you?"

"OH MY GOD!!! All the time!" I heard a real sense of relief in her voice.

"How does it make you feel?"

"Horrible. Like a piece of meat."

We talked about the problem for a long time. At the end of the conversation I had really mixed feelings. On one hand, I felt better that I was not the only person who suffered this kind of treatment. On the other hand, I felt a lot worse, because not only did I have to deal with this, but now I realized that my students—middle-school girls—were being catcalled on the street by men who were probably at least twice their age. This, I decided, was NOT COOL. I had to do something about it.

I could tell that Lara felt a lot better about being called out just from talking about it with me; at least she knew that it was okay to complain. Even though the things being yelled to her were supposedly compliments, she didn't have to think of them as flattery. Lara told some of her friends about our conversation, and over the next few days I had similar talks with a number of other students.

I realized that the girls felt better simply because they had someone to share their feelings with, even though we didn't really resolve anything. I felt better too, because these conversations—even though they didn't stop the catcalling—were helping my students deal with the problem, if only by letting the girls know it was okay to be upset by the comments.

"I think I was in seventh grade when a man in a car first honked at me. The sad thing is, I didn't feel disgusted at first. In fact, maybe I was a little excited, because I never thought I got any special attention from guys. Now I am sixteen years old, and there isn't one day that I can walk down the street and not get honked at or catcalled. I mostly just ignore it, because I know that whatever I do or say back to them won't make the situation better.

"Recently, my eleven-year-old sister told me about an experience she had when walking down the street with my twenty-six-year-old cousin. While walking home, a group of young teenage boys approached them. 'Hey beautifuls,' they said, 'can we talk to you?' When my sister and cousin continued walking, the group of boys called them bitches, and left them alone. My sister came home angry and embarrassed, because she had never experienced sexual harassment on the street before. When I told her that it would start to happen a lot, she got mad at me and slammed the door to her room." Olivia, 16

## Responding to catcalls

This is a really difficult subject for me to talk about, because I am conflicted about what advice I want to offer. On one hand, I want you to feel empowered, to feel like you don't have to listen to guys talk to you in this degrading way. And when they do, you have the right to tell them off. On the other hand, I think it can be dangerous for young girls to mouth off to older men on the street. I wouldn't want you to say something that might result in someone retaliating, either verbally or physically.

I think there are some situations in which it is safe to respond. If you are being called out by someone you know, especially someone your age, you can tell him that you don't appreciate his behavior, not to mention that it makes him sound like an idiot.

If you are with an adult, you might ask him or her to say something to your catcaller. I once stood up for my students at a baseball game when a bunch of guys twice their age made some inappropriate remarks. I told the guys how young the girls were, and they felt like fools. But I think that if my students had said something to them, the guys would have taken it as a cue to be even more inappropriate.

As a general rule, I'd say that it is best to keep quiet and walk with your head up. You know who you are and what you deserve. Anyone who is going to talk to you this way isn't worth even a little bit of your energy.

During one of these talks, a girl said, "Wouldn't it be great if we could do this as a mini-term class?" (The school where I was working had a six-week term in the middle of the year during which all regular classes were suspended, and teachers taught whatever electives they wanted.) I also thought it would be great, as did my principal. I opened a class only for girls, devoted to discussing issues that affected them. The class was called, "Help... I'm a Teenage Girl!"

**My teenage brain**

Teaching this class reminded me how hard it had been to be an adolescent girl. As I listened to my students talk about their lives, I realized that I had forgotten how it really felt to be a teenager. I felt as if people were judging me all the time, and that no matter what I did, I was doing something wrong. I once saw a scene on TV where a girl was talking to her dad. She was about fourteen or fifteen, and was telling him that she could never imagine feeling more stressed out than she did then.

"Sweetheart," he said, "you've never been through medical school. Just wait."
"Dad," she said, "you've never been a teenage girl!"

The girl's words stuck in my head. There was a lot of truth in what she said. I've had plenty of experiences in my life, and I've felt lots of stress. But no time in my life was tougher than being a teenager. I have never felt more insecure about myself, my body, or my social life.

Every day something would change in my circle of friends. I never knew who was going to be my enemy. It was impossible to know if people were talking about me behind my back, so I always assumed they were, and I didn't trust anyone. No matter what clothes I wore, I just couldn't get comfortable in my skin. And my parents, the people who were supposed to love me and care for me the most, seemed to make everything worse. They didn't get what was going on in my head, and it seemed like all they did was criticize me. I felt like I had no one to talk to about my problems. I was alone. It was me against the world. And it sucked.

That's why I'm writing this book. It's hard to be a teenage girl. For adolescents, insecurity is a way of life. As an adolescent, I found it impossible to shake the feeling that I was being judged about every little thing I said or did, because I myself was judging everyone else. Too often, girls deal with their insecurities by treating other girls badly. Girls can judge each other mercilessly, and can be brutally mean. Too often, instead of cooperating, girls compete. We need to support each other instead of putting one another down.

**Living in a supermodel world**

As women, we already get enough messages telling us that we are second-class citizens. We live in a society where women are often treated like objects: things to be seen and touched, not people to be respected and loved. Advertisements use sex to sell stuff, from music to movies to beer to clothes to anything else you can possibly imagine. The female body is beautiful, and its beauty is exploited to make money. Few people stop to think about how this exploitation affects our society, particularly our young women, many of whom already suffer from pretty high levels of insecurity.

## Stressed out!

**6:30 AM** Wake up. Yuck!

**6:31 AM** Look in the mirror. Yuck again.

**6:35 AM** Into the shower. Can't go to school with my hair looking like this.

**6:45 AM** Begin the blow-drying process.

**6:55 AM** Finish the blow-drying process. My hair looks the same as when I woke up. Damn!

**7:00 AM** Get dressed. I feel like I look fat in everything.

**7:10 AM** Change my entire outfit. For the third time.

**7:20 AM** Mom starts harassing me about breakfast. I tell her I can't eat because I need to finish my homework.

Work furiously on stupid math assignment. I don't get it at all. It's giving me a headache.

**7:30 AM** Leave for school. Dad gives me a ride. I get out a block before school because I am embarrassed that my dad is driving me and I don't have any cool friends with cars to give me a ride.

**7:40 AM** Get to school. The day has hardly begun and I am already stressed, with a headache to top it off. And what do I have first period? Gym! By the end of the period, my hair will look worse than it did when I woke up. And I'll have to change clothes in front of all the other girls in the locker room. Twice.

How many times have you looked at a model in a magazine and wished that you looked like her? I know that I've done it maybe...a million times. At least! I've pasted photos of models on my refrigerator in hopes that seeing the pictures would discourage me from eating. I've stood naked in front of the mirror and held the magazine pictures up next to me, looking at all the places where my body was different from the woman's body in the picture.

Basically, I've tortured myself with those stupid model pictures. WHY? I am a normal woman who wears a size 10 or 12 (like most women, even though 10 or 12 is not the middle of the size scale), and I have curvy hips and a round butt and a little extra flab all over. But I really don't care. I know that this is who I am, and I am okay with it. I can't say I've felt that way my whole life. I can't even say I feel that way all the time now. I'm forty-two years old, and I have only started to feel this way in the past few years. I can't tell you how many silly diets I've tried, how much exercise I've done, how much time I've spent feeling bad about my body. The truth is, I might as well love it. What other choice do I have?

Why has it been so difficult for me to feel good about how I look? The expectations society has of us are unrealistic, and lead us to dislike ourselves and the way we look. I am sorry that our society is that way. I really am. I know how it makes you feel, because it wasn't too long ago that I felt that way myself all the time, and I still feel that way sometimes. I wish I could make the women in the media look more like most women in the world. That will take time. What I can do now, though, is try to help you deal with the insecurities you are facing and try to combat all these challenging social influences by helping you feel better about yourself.

## Your assignment is...

Now, I know you don't want to have to do any more (gasp!) homework, but this book requires a small assignment. Pick up any magazine. Take it with you to a nearby store or coffee shop, or any place where there are a lot of people. Now sit and people-watch for a while. As you people-watch, notice the women you see. On a piece of paper, make two columns—one for women who look like the women in the magazine, one for those who don't. Keep doing this until you've seen a hundred women. Now look at your piece of paper. Unless you are playing this game at a supermodel party or a photo shoot, I can guarantee that less than half of the women you see look like the women in the magazine.

## Positive thinking

First of all, you should know that it is normal to feel somewhat insecure and unsure of yourself. You are going through a tough time, during which it can seem as if everything about you is wrong. It's easy to be negative about yourself when the pictures of beauty you see don't look like you. It's even easier to be negative about yourself when it feels like your friends are judging the way you look and act every day. The truth is, though, that they are judging and criticizing because they share the same insecurities. I'm not sure that helps you, but at least keep it in mind the next time you feel bad about yourself because of something a friend says. She's probably saying it because she feels bad about herself.

In this book, I try to be honest with you about what I've learned about being a teenage girl. I've learned these things from my own life as well as from the experiences of my students. I'm sharing them with you because I think that we can do much better. We don't have to feel insecure, and we certainly don't have to compete with the women around us to feel better about ourselves. We can feel good about ourselves, and be proud of the strong, beautiful, interesting, capable, young women we are. I hope my words can help you do just that.

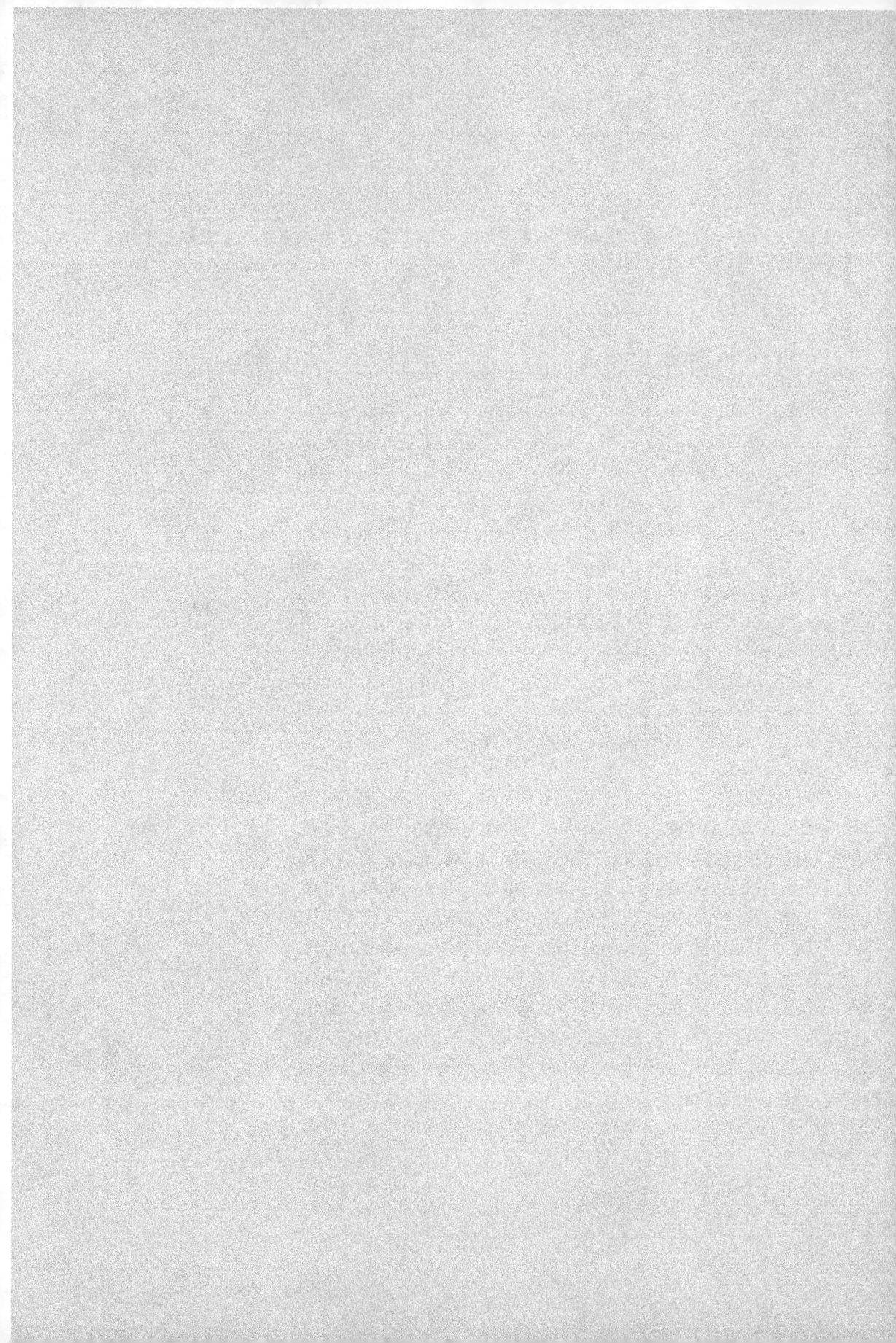

ONE

# That Crazy Teenage World

I have a thirteen-year-old cousin whom I think of as my little sister. We hang out when we can; I help her with her homework, and we gossip about what's going on in our lives. I've known her since she was little, and I've watched her grow up over the years. She's a special girl with a unique spirit—one of those kids who's nice to everyone and makes friends pretty easily. Over the past year or so, she's changed a lot. She fidgets more—seems less comfortable in her own skin, almost as if someone is making her wear a suit that doesn't fit. She's less willing to give me a hug in public when she sees me, and is easily embarrassed, especially by her parents' behavior. She's short tempered, especially with those who love her the most, and sometimes bursts into fits of anger. I can tell that even she isn't sure where all this behavior is coming from. It suddenly dawned on me. Oh yeah! She's entering the world of adolescence.

## My adolescence

Watching my cousin's behavior, I remember myself in middle school. I was the same way. I went from being a super-confident, happy, well-adjusted person to feeling as if I was walking on nails all the time. Nothing I could say or do was right in my eyes. I felt uncomfortable in my body and was sure everything I wore looked bad. At school, I would say stuff and my so-called friends would laugh at me. At camp, girls made

"I feel like I will never fit in. No matter what I do."
Nora, 14

## What is adolescence?[1]

Adolescence is the stage of development between childhood and adulthood.
It begins when you enter puberty. The term puberty refers to all the physical
changes that happen inside and outside your body as it transforms itself
into an adult's body.

During puberty, you experience lots of changes:

> PHYSICALLY, you'll begin to look more like an adult. You will also be able to
get pregnant and have babies, because you will be menstruating, or getting
your period. Getting your period is a sign that your body is producing eggs,
which are what get fertilized by sperm to make you pregnant.

> MENTALLY, you will be able to make more decisions for yourself, but you
might also feel more stressed out and anxious than you used to.

> SOCIALLY, you may feel the need for friends more than ever, and you also
might try out new interests and hobbies.

fun of me. I was once even in a cabin where all the girls called
me "Annoy Me" instead of Naomi. Our counselor did too! It
was horrible. I didn't know why all this was happening, but I
felt really self-conscious, like people were scrutinizing every
move I made. And actually, I really wasn't such an outcast or
anything—I was fun, cool, and interesting—but I definitely
didn't think that about myself at the time.

The worst part about the whole thing was that my parents,
who loved me and supported me more completely than anyone,
couldn't help me out at all, and in fact made everything worse.

My parents were cool; I mean, really, they were. They were pretty lenient and didn't nag me too much about things most parents get upset about. They trusted me to do my homework and keep my stuff neat. They let me hang out with my friends when I wanted to, and gave me the freedom to do what I liked.

Yet somehow, as I look back on being in middle and high school, one of my clearest memories is of fighting with my parents. I argued with them about everything. It didn't really matter what it was. If I was in a mood and they crossed my path, it was war. I would get into these yelling bouts with them, which never went well. By the end, I was usually crying, and had no clue why we'd started fighting in the first place.

I was a mess and had no idea why. I really didn't get it. On the outside, it seemed like I should be a well-adjusted person—I did well in school, was fairly popular, and had a loving, supportive family. Yet despite all those things, I was full of rage and took most of it out on my parents. I pushed away the very people I needed the most.

Does it seem totally counterproductive to push away people who love you by fighting with them and making yourself and them unhappy? It was! My behavior was not rational at all. But it was very typical for an adolescent.

"My parents drive me nuts. My mom is always in my face and is really uppity about my schoolwork. I wish she would just leave me alone."

Liza, 13

Adolescence is a crazy time for everyone. Generally, your temper is shorter. Often, you have less patience and a lower threshold for frustration. It's difficult to concentrate, and really easy to get very worked up about things that may seem meaningless later.

Life feels different. Things that once seemed important have become childish, and nothing is as simple as it used to be. And what's worse is that it seems no one gets who you are or what you are going through. I remember that almost every time I would fight with my parents, I'd yell at them: "You just don't understand me!" And I never thought they took me seriously. Actually, they did know that I was going through an intense time. I was the one who didn't understand. My brain and body were changing, and as a result, I was having a hard time finding my place in the world around me.

In many ways, as an adolescent it can feel like you are living multiple lives. On one hand, you are the person you are inside. You are going through lots of changes and have thoughts that confuse you. One second you're happy and life is good; the next second you're mad at the world and everything anyone says upsets you. One second it seems like nothing can go wrong, then the next you are crying and you can't even understand why. On the other hand, you are the person you are on the outside, and this person changes depending on who is around. We act differently when we are around our friends and when we are spending time with our parents. It's all very overwhelming and confusing.

## Hormones

It might help to know that these feelings are normal, that they are pretty much the result of lots of hormones surging through your body. Hormones pulse through our bodies at different times for different reasons. When we are born, certain hormones tell the body how it should grow. When we get really excited about something, a hormone called adrenaline makes us feel energetic. Hormones really kick into gear in adolescence, when your body goes through a lot of physical changes.

As a result of these changes in hormones, our emotional reactions change too. Hormones that cause physical changes affect our emotions and the ways in which we react to situations. For example, about the time you get your period, the change in hormone levels can result in you feeling more moody than usual.

In general, during adolescence you no longer respond to things in the same way as you used to. Your image of yourself changes too. This, I think, is a crucial challenge for adolescents, especially adolescent girls. We can become really self conscious

## What are hormones?[2]

Hormones are basically chemical messengers your body creates and sends out to tell different parts of your body to do things. The hormones that most affect teens during adolescence are the reproductive hormones, the messengers that get the body ready to have babies. In girls, the main reproductive hormone is called estrogen. In boys, it is called testosterone.

Estrogen and testosterone have a big impact on behavior as well as body shape. These hormones basically fuel the transformation from being a child into being a sexual adult. There is no "right" time for puberty to begin, though in girls it tends to happen between the ages of eleven and fourteen.

In girls, estrogen stimulates growth of the womb and breasts. Estrogen also changes the woman's body by rearranging where fat is stored. This is why girls become curvier during puberty. Fat that used to be stored around your stomach might be moved to your breasts, butt, or hips.

In boys, testosterone contributes to shaping the body. Boys often become leaner and have greater capacity to build muscle. This is why guys who were once skinny and lanky might come back from summer break one year looking like men—taller and more muscular, with broader shoulders. Testosterone also promotes the growth of body hair in boys. After puberty, boys can grow facial hair.

Estrogen and testosterone don't simply cause physical changes that allow the body to reproduce. They also have a psychological impact, making you more interested in sex than you were before. This is the body's way of making you want to reproduce. Sexual feelings during adolescence are totally normal. You can read more about this in Chapter Seven.

and it becomes much easier to see ourselves negatively than positively, even though being positive will likely make us much happier.

Before adolescence, I was generally happy and felt good about myself, but occasionally I'd come up against a bump in the road that would make me unhappy. During adolescence, I was down on myself much of the time, and only sometimes did I feel good about myself.

## Feeling insecure?

At the same time as your self-image is changing, so is everyone else's. The other kids around you—boys and girls—are going through similar changes, and face the same insecurities that you do. Unfortunately, one of the main ways people deal with their own insecurities is to knock other people down. For some people, it's easier to feel okay about yourself if you think you are better than the person next to you, or at least if you make her think you are better than she is. Think about it, and be honest with yourself: how many times have you made someone else feel bad in an attempt to make yourself feel better? Even if doing this doesn't actually make you feel that much better, at least on the outside it looks like success.

"I have hurt people by talking about them. I guess it's like the more flaws I uncover about someone else, the more perfect I am. When I say things to people in front of their faces it helps me break them down into how little and insignificant I want them to be."
Jelani, 13

## Dealing with stress[3]

Stress can be really overwhelming and even incapacitating at times. If you are so stressed out that you can't think straight, it can seem like there is no way out of the vicious stress cycle. Here are some strategies to deal with stress:

**> Exercise!** Exercising releases hormones into the body that motivate you and make you feel good about yourself. Sometimes, going for a run or a swim or even just stretching will help calm you down.

**> Breathe!** Taking really deep breaths and holding them for a few seconds will, without a doubt, relax you. When you really breathe in as deeply as you can and hold it, your body has a natural physical response that makes you relax, even if your mind is crowded with stressful thoughts. Try to sit still and focus just on breathing for a little while. It will take your mind off your stress and allow you to release.

**> Relax!** There are techniques that you can learn (or just figure out on your own) that will help you relax your muscles. Lie down in a comfortable position and try to notice what parts of your body are tense.

Think about relaxing your body, starting with your face and jaw. Then relax your shoulders, arms, and back. Work your way all the way down to your toes and lie there for a while, letting your muscles just loosen up.

**> Visualize!** Imagine yourself somewhere that makes you feel calm and relaxed. I always go to the beach in my mind when I do this, but you should choose whatever place works for you. Think about being there, and enjoy.

**> Laugh!** Spend time with people who make you smile; read a book that will crack you up. Laughter is the best medicine life has to offer.

So as everyone becomes more insecure, it might be that they also become meaner and more willing to cut other people down. Working with adolescents, I see this behavior all the time. Dirty looks are often more frequent than smiles. Insults are thrown around much more than compliments. Too often, competition takes the place of cooperation. So not only are we feeling insecure because our self-image is changing, but we are also under an UNBELIEVABLE AMOUNT OF STRESS.

## Why girls? Why me?

While this behavior is common among both boys and girls, I find that meanness and competition affect girls in a far worse way than boys. Women and girls are more aware of social hierarchies than men and boys are. When I say social hierarchies (pronounced HEYE-ur-ar-keez), I mean the way that cliques and social groups are structured. We'll get into this more in Chapter Four, but just to give you a brief idea—in every social group, there are some people who are leaders and others who are not. Inside that, there are different ways in which people respond to each other, depending on how much they respect one another.

## Rungs on the ladder[4]

In her book *Queen Bees and Wannabes: Helping Your Daughter Survive Cliques, Gossip, Boyfriends, and Other Realities of Adolescence*, Rosalind Wiseman breaks down the teen-girl social ladder as she sees it. I am not sure if I agree with all of what she says, but I think it's interesting to think about her ideas. The following quotations are from her book.

### > The Queen Bee

This is the girl who is the leader of her clique. "Through a combination of charisma, force, money, looks, will, and manipulation, this girl reigns supreme over the other girls and weakens their friendships with others, thereby strengthening her own power and influence. Never underestimate her power over other girls (and boys as well). She can and will silence her peers with a look."

### > The Sidekick

The girl who hangs with the queen bee all the time. "She's the lieutenant or second in command, the girl who's closest to the queen bee and will back her no matter what because her power depends on the confidence she gets from the queen bee."

### > The Banker

This girl doesn't bank money, she banks information and knows how powerful that information can be. "The banker creates chaos everywhere she goes by banking information about girls in her social sphere and dispensing it at strategic intervals for her own benefit. For instance, if a girl has said something negative about another girl, the banker will casually mention it to someone in conversation because she knows it is going to cause conflict and strengthen her status as someone in the know."

### > The Floater

This girl isn't really bound to only one clique. "She has friends in different groups and can move freely among them."

### > The Torn Bystander

This is the girl who sees mean behavior for what it is, but isn't sure whether to say something to the perpetrators. "She's constantly conflicted between doing the right thing and her allegiance to the clique. As a result, she's the one most likely to be caught in the middle of a conflict between two girls or groups of girls."

> ### The Pleaser/Wannabe/Messenger

This girl is trying her hardest to get "in," no matter what. "Almost all girls are pleasers/wannabes, some are just more obvious than others... [The pleaser] will do anything to be in the good graces of the queen bee and the sidekick. She'll mimic their clothes, style, and anything else she thinks will increase her position in the group."

> ### The Target

This girl is exactly who she sounds like she is: the target for ridicule. "She's the victim, set up by the other girls to be humiliated, made fun of, excluded.... Often, the social hierarchy of the clique is maintained precisely by having someone clearly at the bottom of the group's totem pole."

Think about your own friends. I would guess that in your circle there are probably one, maybe two, girls who kind of tell the others what to do. They might not give instructions directly or anything like that, but they do know that other girls listen to them. They have power, they know it, and other people recognize it too.

Usually, in middle and high school, this power is based on popularity. The more popular you are, the more power you have. But even inside the most popular clique, there are girls who don't have any power; they do what the leaders of their clique expect them to do.

The point is that different people have different amounts of power, and as a result have different places on the social ladder. Girls tend to be much more aware of this ordering of people than boys are. Girls are much more likely to compete for positions of power, and more likely to criticize others to make themselves look better. I think that meanness and competition are among the biggest challenges girls have to face during adolescence.

It hurts when your friends turn on you, and it's impossible to predict when it's going to happen. I could fill this whole book with stories my students have told me about being treated badly by their 'friends.' Countless girls have come in to school one day to find that their friends are not speaking to them anymore. Lots of girls have spoken of conference-calling people (or being called themselves) to gossip about others who are secretly on the other line listening to the entire conversation. I could print an entire book of mean comments posted on social media. It's not easy to feel good about yourself when the people whom you think like you simply decide to stab you in the back when it is convenient. And, honestly, we know it could happen at any time because as much as we hate to admit it, chances are we would do it to our own friends if we needed to. That's the harsh reality.

## Fitting in

This problem is made even worse for girls when we look at the unrealistic images society creates for women. In the last chapter, I asked you to compare images of women in the media with real women you see on the street. You and I both know that these images of women are unrealistic ideals for most of us, yet at the same time, we hold them in our heads as the ones we want to copy. When girls criticize each other using these idealized images as standards, they are falling into a vicious cycle that hurts girls in a big way.

Often, girls feel like they have to look and act a certain way to fit a particular image. Usually, the image that girls think they have to copy is quite different from who they really are, and they find themselves acting in ways that are foreign to them, and may even make them really uncomfortable.

"Images affect how we act and dress. Girls my age in particular are going through a stage of uncertainty and just want to fit in. Trying to be like the images we see, especially in the media, seems like the perfect way to fit in. I think the media shows us as brainless, pretty objects for boys to boss around and have sex with." Jelani, 13

We'll get deeper into all of these things in later chapters, but I just want to make sure you understand how this cycle works. If you can see what the forces are behind the stresses you are experiencing, you will be better prepared to deal with them.

So, just to recap:

> Hormones result in physical and psychological changes in adolescence. These physical and psychological changes affect your self-image, and all of a sudden it is harder to feel good about yourself; often the default position is to be self-critical.

> As you are becoming self-critical, so is everyone else your age. Often, the way people deal with that is to criticize and judge others.

> Girls tend to be both more aware of social hierarchies and more outwardly mean and verbally aggressive toward their friends than boys. Feeling insecure, we treat our friends badly and make them feel even worse. (This works both ways—most people are usually on both the giving and receiving ends of this treatment.)

> A great deal of the criticism and judgment girls dish out is based on whether their peers fit an image of an ideal. This image is created by the media, and is unrealistic for most women, much less girls, to achieve.

> In the quest to achieve this unrealistic image, girls put themselves in a whole bunch of situations that make them uncomfortable. In trying to achieve the ideal, girls experience huge challenges, all connected to acting like (and often believing that) it is more important to fit an image than to be themselves.

**What can you do about it?**

I know it seems like I am saying that there are fifty million things wrong with the world. I'm sure that solving all these problems seems pretty overwhelming. It is. As much as I wish this was not the case, I don't think society is going to completely turn around in your lifetime. Instead, I hope to help you change, so that you are better prepared to deal with the world around you. While we might not be able to change all of what is happening around us, we can change the way things affect us by changing the way we see ourselves. We can also be an example for others who are trying to do the same. So, I want to offer you some suggestions to help you deal with all the craziness around you and in your head. Remember, these are only suggestions; no one is forcing you to try any of these things. But like anything else, you can't know if something will work for you unless you really check it out. If you've given something a fair try and it still isn't working for you, drop it. Some of my suggestions will be useless for some people, for sure. But you won't know which might work for you if you don't try!

***

First and foremost, **be true to the self in your heart**. This is your inner self. She knows the difference between when you are acting the way you want to and when you are doing something because someone else expects you to. She knows that sometimes you do stuff because you feel pressure from the outside, but she doesn't judge you for that. She sometimes gets upset, though, because she worries that you might be too influenced by external pressures, and wants you to remember who you are. She wants you to keep an eye on what makes you happy, so that you don't compromise too much when you are faced with stresses from the outside.

I find that it can be very difficult to be true to my inner self. It's hard to know what I really want to do. When I was an adolescent it was especially hard for me to tell the difference between what my inner self wanted and what she thought she wanted based on the expectations other people had of me. To help you identify the difference between what you want and what other people may think you want, and to help clear your head in general, I suggest that you **write in a journal**. I find that when thoughts are mixed up in my head, it really helps me to organize them by writing them down. I can at least start to make sense of all the ideas swimming around in my brain. I think that writing in a journal can be really useful anytime that life overwhelms you. Do it whenever you feel like it. Maybe your journal is something you bust out once a week or once a month, or maybe you write in it every day. Maybe you write when you're upset, maybe when you're happy, or maybe when you're feeling like no one is listening to you. It's your call. In journal writing, there is only one rule: express yourself. Write however you want. Your journal is for your eyes only, unless you decide to share it. It's not for school, so there's no need to write in complete sentences, no need to censor yourself, or to think about how anyone else might react to what you are saying. If you want to get really into it, make or buy yourself a cool book that you can use as your journal, something you're proud of, a worthy place to store your thoughts.

I also suggest that you **read over your journal** once in a while. This will allow you to reflect on how you or someone else behaved in a situation once you have some distance from it. Looking back in your journal can help you think about whether you respect the way you acted or reacted to something once you are no longer having intense emotions about it. You can evaluate your own behavior, and think about whether you did things to make yourself feel better or worse. It will also allow you to think about your friends' behavior, and whether they acted in ways that were helpful or hurtful. Thinking about these things can help you deal better with similar situations in the future.

\*\*\*

When you read over your journal, and just in general, **notice the language you use to talk about yourself**. Language has power. If I speak about myself in positive, encouraging language, I empower myself, even when I am talking about something I want to change. There is a difference between saying, "I am the slowest runner in our class!" and, "I know that I can run faster. I am going to work on it." Both statements refer to the same thing, but the second has a positive spin to it, and it has action in it—it empowers me to do something. Of course, I am not going to be the best at everything I do, but that doesn't mean I should talk about myself negatively. The language we use affects how we experience things and how we see ourselves.

Speak with words that strengthen and inspire you. I also want to suggest that, aside from journal writing, you **find a way to express yourself**. Pick an activity you like to do. It can be anything that makes you happy—art, music, dance, sports, or whatever. Try to do this activity on a regular basis. If you build something like this into your routine, you will be helping yourself on many levels.

The time you spend doing this activity will be a time for you to focus on doing something that makes you happy. If you have this opportunity once a week or once a day or however often you can fit it in, you will be able to look forward to this time, and know that it will make you feel good, no matter what else might be going on in your life.

Take this activity to the next level. Don't be satisfied with knowing that you are making the time to dance, for example; push yourself to become an even better dancer. (Always remember, you are improving for yourself, in relation to yourself. You don't have to compete with others to improve, only with yourself, each day trying to do better than YOU did yesterday.) Take a dance class and try your hardest to be the best dancer you can be. If you love to play soccer, join a team and challenge yourself to learn as much as you can to improve your game. The more you challenge yourself, the better you'll feel about your accomplishments. Not to mention that you will be improving your skills at something you love, which will help you enjoy that activity even more.

Finally, and perhaps most important, **make time for yourself**. This is different from the time you spend doing your activity. This is your own solo thinking time. It is unbelievable how overscheduled we are these days. It is essential that you make sure to have a little bit of time for yourself, even just five minutes, every day. This is your time—for you to think about whatever you want, or do whatever you want. This time is for you to ignore anything that might be preventing you from doing your thing, to ignore anything that might be getting in the way of you simply being who you are.

It's important to remember that, despite all the pressures you are feeling, you still need a bit of quiet to keep your brain in order, to think about who you are and what makes you happy, and to just generally value yourself.

\*\*\*

And, my friends, it is that last one that is most important— if you value yourself and always remember that you are important, you will be able to get through anything, even adolescence. Give yourself at least a moment to remember that every day.

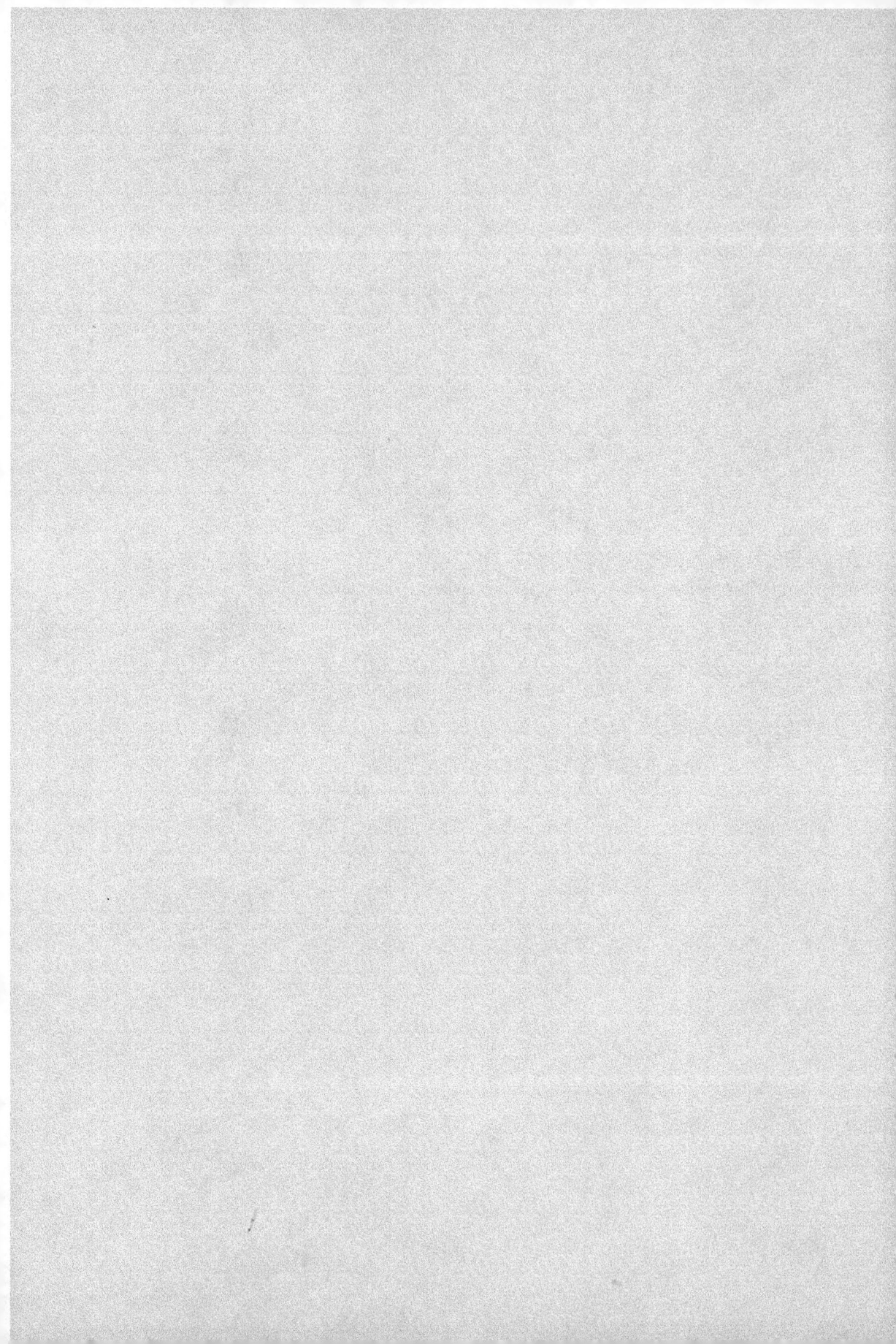

TWO

# Don't Question Yourself—
# Question the Media!

I don't watch much TV, but a bunch of years ago a friend and I got really into reality shows. We loved to talk trash about the characters as their dramatic lives unfolded on-screen. At the same time, I couldn't help but notice that all the things I objected to so passionately were being flaunted on TV. Girls dressed in skimpy clothing went out at night and got drunk and flirted with boys, who sometimes got them in trouble and always got their attention. Don't get me wrong—the guys were hot for a lot of girls throughout the season, and had their fair share of adventures. But the main difference between the boys' escapades and the girls' was that when the boys went out, they still had all their clothes on.

While I admit that I enjoyed the show and watched it whenever I could, I was bothered by the fact that the camera's perspective on the girls shifted craftily between cool, interesting women I might enjoy hanging out with and objects of desire wearing little clothing and attracting lots of attention.

I think we can all admit that the female body is beautiful, and for centuries artists have tried to capture its beauty on canvas, in stone, or in photographs. The Mona Lisa, Venus de Milo, and hundreds of other famous works of art have represented images of femininity over the centuries. I would even go so far as to say that the female body is more pleasing to the eye than the male body, if only because the male body seems so functional, while the female form is more like an artistically rendered sculpture. Yet so many of the modern images we see of women are not created to glorify the female form; instead, they exploit its appeal to sell things.

What TV and so many other sources have so blatantly pointed out to me is that we use the beauty of the female body to our advantage. I've seen tons of ads that feature women with huge breasts, wearing bikinis, and smiling flirtatiously, even though they have nothing to do with the actual product. Advertisers use these images to make ads that will get people to buy whatever they can—beer, a car, or even a pair of glasses. Now don't get me wrong: this goes both ways. There are tons of ads that feature attractive men posing in various positions to sell whatever their products are. There are far more images like that of women, though. And the women tend to be wearing less clothing.

If you remember, I got the idea to write this book from teaching a young women's empowerment program in various schools around the country. In my class, we do a homework assignment that I would like you to do as well.

**Your assignment is...**

Make a Collage. Collect as many photographs of women as you can find in ads, and gather them together in a digital or paper collage.

Now look carefully at the pictures you see. I am obviously not looking at those photos myself, but I am willing to make a few guesses about what you are seeing in front of you. I am pretty sure you are looking at a lot of nearly naked women, most of whose bodies are fairly unhealthy. They are too thin for their frames and, in my collage at least, most of these women are making suggestive faces, trying to look like they are waiting for sex.

In a recent class in which we looked at students' collages, Nicole noticed that in her collage, all the women had the same expression. They were pouting, with their lips sort of open and their eyes half closed, looking sleepy and suggestive. When I asked her why she thought the models were making these faces, she told me she thought they must have been doing it to look sexy because, she said, "Sex sells."

Do these women really want the people who look at the ads to want to have sex with them, or are they making these faces because someone else is telling them to? While the women are choosing to be part of these ads, I think we can be pretty sure that there are other people behind the scenes who tell the models what they should look like, just like there are people who tell them what to wear.

In these ads, I don't think the models are meant to be seen as real people with feelings. Instead, they are portrayed as objects, like statues, there to be looked at, not talked to. Granted, we are talking about ads here, which are meant to evoke one feeling—I want that! So, in order to make us want to buy what they are selling, advertisers use pictures to make us think that we will be as cool/beautiful/sexy as the woman we see if we buy the product in the ad. Or that she'll want to have sex with us—we will become the object of her desire. Either way, she's a tool the advertisers use to sell us something.

### In the name of beauty

Ninety-two percent of plastic surgery procedures done in the US in 2014 were performed on women. These procedures included, but were not limited to, the following:

- Abdominoplasty—aka, tummy tuck • Breast augmentation—aka, implants
- Breast lift • Breast reduction • Buttock implants • Buttock lift • Face-lift
- Lip implant • Liposuction • Rhinoplasty—aka, nose job • Chemical peels
- Laser hair removal • Botox

## What is objectification?

I could write a whole other book about advertising and all the problems it causes, especially for teenagers. But for now, let's focus seriously on what it means to see women as objects, because I think the fact that we do has a pretty deep impact on you. I think it's really important for us to understand how seeing women as objects affects our society—especially how it affects teenage girls—so that we can deal with it.

The practice of objectification, seeing people as objects rather than as people, is so much a part of our culture that most of us, guys especially, don't even think twice about it. I have many male friends who are kind, considerate people, who won't bat an eyelash before they check out some girl's body and comment about it. This is not to say that women don't do this as well! I am the first to admit that I will look twice at an attractive guy who passes me on the street.

But, I think that objectification has a particularly harsh impact on women, both because women are objectified more often than men, and also because the images we see of ideal women are so often unrealistic for most women to achieve. These media images set up a standard of beauty that makes many women painfully self-critical, especially about our bodies. These images also make adolescent girls, who are trying so hard to fit in, feel like the way to fit in is to look and act like the women they see on TV and online.

## Who makes the rules?

On the opening day of my class, I always ask my students to talk about what they want to discuss during our time together. In one class, Nina said she wanted to talk about rules. She asked, "What is appropriate for us? I mean, what is appropriate for us to be doing with boys? What are the rules about how we should be?" Hands shot up around the circle.

Girls responded by telling her that she had to make her own rules. There are always going to be people who will tell you what to do, her peers told her, but it is up to you to decide whether you are going to listen to them. Parents and teachers will happily tell you what they think is right. TV and movies give us ideas about what might make us happy, and how we should look and act if we want to get there. All around us there are influences telling us how to behave. Our culture has lots of different ways of telling us what the rules are; it's up to each of us individually to make sense of what we see. I know it's tough, but if you don't, then you are lost in a sea of influences. That's pretty much what life can feel like—a sea of influences; images coming from all over the place, images that tell you what you should look like, how you should act, who you should talk to, how you should live. It's up to you to sort through those influences and figure out which ones you want to listen to and which you want to ignore. People can tell you which to choose, but ultimately, you are going to have to decide for yourself. This is especially hard to do when you are trying to fit in and there are so many different sets of rules coming at you from so many different places. But the more you are able to define what's right for you, the happier you will be, and the better prepared you will be to respond to the all the influences swirling around you.

## Am I an object?

I think there are two important questions we need to ask:

> How does the exploitation of women's looks affect us?
> How can we handle it?

I can speak best from my own experience. I am generally a happy, well-adjusted person, but I can't help but compare myself to what society sees as the ideal image of female beauty. I know I will never be five feet ten and super skinny. But I do wish every once in a while that I was a little thinner, that my skin was a little more perfect, that my hips were a little narrower, that my arms were a little less flabby—I could go on forever.

"White women are considered the prettiest of all. Girls want to look like the white image. You don't have to be mixed to have nice hair. You are beautiful. Everybody is beautiful in their own way. How can you let someone else tell you what is beautiful?" Aisha, 12

We all look at ourselves this way to an extent. Think about it: how many times have you looked at someone on TV or in a magazine or on the Internet and wished you looked like her? I've definitely done it. It's normal to feel that way. Cultures have an image of beauty that represents an ideal. People who grow up in that culture are taught to believe that this image is the standard by which we should judge ourselves and others.

**Truth in the *Twilight Zone***

There is a famous *Twilight Zone* episode that opens with a gorgeous woman lying on a surgery table, with lots of hands poking and prodding her as she is being examined. The doctor's voice is in the background, and he is talking about the woman's upcoming procedure, which is going to be some kind of plastic surgery on her face. The doctor seems unsure as to whether the surgery is going to be successful, but the woman decides to go ahead with it anyway.

The surgery happens, and she returns to the doctor's office two weeks later to have her bandages removed. She's lying on the surgery table, and again the doctor's voice is in the background. We haven't seen his face yet. The doctor reminds her that they may not have succeeded, and not to be too disappointed at the results.

The entire time, I am wondering, "What could this woman possibly want to change about herself?" She seems perfect to me. She is strikingly beautiful. What would she want to alter about her appearance?

In the final scene, the doctor's hands remove the woman's bandages, and she looks exactly the same as she did in the first scene, as beautiful as ever. The doctors all seem very sorry and disappointed, and try to reassure the woman. The camera finally pans out to reveal the doctors' faces; they all look like pigs.

Why did I mention this episode? Think about it! What is it telling us about the culture we live in? There is a mainstream standard of beauty. People define themselves and others as beautiful based on how closely they can imitate the standard. People who feel that they don't fit that standard—which is the majority of people, when the ideal represents such a narrow portion of the population—will go to great lengths to try to achieve the ideal.

"Images of beauty affect every race. If I look at a magazine, most of the people I see are white. I am Latina. The images in the magazines affect me because they are saying that all women have to look that way. Too many Latina women think their bodies should look like white people's bodies." Monica, 17

## In search of the perfect body[2]

Just to have a sense of how unrealistic our ideal of the perfect female body is, consider the fact that most fashion models are thinner than 98 percent of American women. The average American woman is five feet four inches tall and weighs 140 pounds. The average American model is five feet eleven and weighs 117 pounds.

## I want to look like...

In one of my classes a number of years ago, my students told me about a TV show in which people get plastic surgery to look like specific celebrities. If that seems a little too over the top to you, consider a show in which women undergo complete personal makeovers so that they can feel better about themselves. They overhaul their bodies with plastic surgery, exercise, and modified eating habits, and try to change their mental state through therapy. These shows really exist! And the women are specifically chosen for the show because they are vulnerable and clearly have a low sense of self-esteem.

Therapy is really important as a means of helping them feel better about themselves, but the primary focus of the show is physical. The women are not allowed to look in the mirror for eight weeks, and each series climaxes at the moment in which they are finally allowed to see their own reflections live on TV. The women literally end up looking like completely different people.

## Image obsession

Our culture is image-obsessed. Too often, we care more about how we look than who we actually are. Don't get me wrong—it's important to take care of yourself; feeling good about your appearance makes you feel better about yourself. Some concern about looks is healthy. I worry about students who come to school looking completely disheveled and out of it. But there is a big difference between caring about how you look and being obsessed with it.

Much of the media that influences adolescent girls tells us that we should be obsessed with our appearances. I am looking at a magazine on my desk. The main headline reads "225 Ways to LOOK REALLY CUTE!" in huge letters that take up a third of the page. Beauty vloggers attract thousands or even millions of viewers who are seeking tips about how to improve their looks.

In middle school and high school, my friends and I read magazines all the time (this was before the Internet...) and I thought nothing of it. We loved doing the quizzes and we admired the models. We religiously did the exercises they suggested so we could have more muscular arms, tighter butts, defined abs, whatever. We bought the beauty products the magazines told us would give us clearer skin, shinier hair, and stronger nails.

"According to the media, beautiful is: thin, clear skin, good body, big boobs, good lips, good makeup. This influences people because they may really want to look like someone, and then they spend money on products that make you 'beautiful,' but are actually just bad for you." Benazir, 13

Looking back, I see that reading these magazines had a much bigger impact on me than I thought at the time. I think that the magazines and the millions of photos we see online encourage us to define ourselves superficially, and then remind us that we don't look like the models, so we will buy the stuff that will help us look like them. It's not the images themselves that I worry about most. What the images encourage people to do is what really concerns me.

"I think the media tells girls that their bodies and looks are the best thing they have going for them—especially in commercials, where they're all like: 'Buy this! Be thinner! Shave with this! Use this lotion to make your skin smooth and beautiful!' It annoys me.

"The standard is to have perfect, skinny, curvy bodies, lots of makeup, long, blond hair, skimpy clothing. I think that image affects a lot of women. It makes me respect people who aren't freakily skinny and still look stunning, like Beyoncé. It affects me, not in a way that makes me feel like I have to be like that, but in a way that makes me annoyed at the image being portrayed." Natalie, 12

If we think back to the cycle I talked about in the last chapter, we can give a context to these media images, and think about what impact they have on our lives. Remember, during adolescence, girls (and boys) are likely to find that their self-image is rapidly changing. You might find yourself feeling insecure and self-

> "Our breasts may be too big, too saggy, too pert, too flat, too full, too far apart, too close together, too A cup, too lopsided, too jiggly, too pale, too padded, too pointy, too pendulous, or just two mosquito bites. But with Dep styling products, at least you can have your hair the way you want it!"
>
> **Dep hair gel ad, late 1980s[3]**

conscious a lot of the time; your peers probably feel the same way. In trying to feel better about ourselves, we cut other people down. Adolescent girls are ruthless about this; girl world is a culture that is permeated with undercover meanness. We've all experienced it. So to avoid being the subject of our friends' cruelty, we try desperately to fit in. We do whatever we can to avoid standing out. Being different from the norm is a red flag for ridicule. If we blend in, we are safely under the radar. So what is the standard? What do we need to do to fit in?

## Selling an image

On some level, the answer to this question comes from the media, which has a tremendous influence on our culture, and bombards people with images all the time. Images are created to sell teens something that will make them fit an ideal. Teens buy into these images, and buy the products associated with them, in the quest to belong.

I recently watched an incredible documentary that breaks down the way the corporate media takes advantage of teenagers. The documentary is called *The Merchants of Cool*; it's a PBS Frontline production, and I highly recommend that you check it out. It's all about how advertising targets teens, largely through MTV, to sell them an image and convince them that if they fit that image, then they will be "cool." The documentary describes how MTV and media in general have created stereotyped caricatures for guys and girls. The idea behind this is that if TV can convince us to want to be like these caricatures, we will be likely to buy the things advertisers are trying to sell us, because the caricatures use the stuff the TV is advertising.

The male image is the "mook"—the perverted, crude guy who is willing to spend endless hours numbing his mind with video games and TV. He's intrigued by vomit and poop, and thinks that talking about farting and boogers is hilarious. He's a lowlife who objectifies women and wants to watch them flaunt their bodies shamelessly whenever and wherever he can. If that happens in the comfort of his home, on the screen, even better. He doesn't have to leave the couch.

## I am sexy; check me out

The female image is the "midriff"—a prematurely adult, sexualized girl who is consumed by her appearance. She learns from the media that being hot (not just pretty, but hot and sexy too) can help her become successful. She knows she can use her looks to be powerful, even if she doesn't understand why. The idols of the midriffs are people like Britney Spears, who blatantly use girlish sexuality to sell music, essentially telling girls, "Your body is your best asset; flaunt your sexuality, even if you don't understand it." The midriff wears skimpy clothes that show off her figure and flirts with everyone to sell her image. Her mantra is, "I am midriff; hear me roar! I am a sexual object, and I am proud of it." In other words, "I know that people are interested in me because of how I look, not because of who I am. But not only am I okay with that, I think it's great."[4]

"At a young age, I don't understand flaunting my sexuality. I would never be caught walking down the street half naked. I think that flaunting your sexuality proves or indicates that some girls feel insecure, and try to cover up their feelings by wearing lots of makeup and clothing that is very revealing." Nicole, 12

Is this who girls really are? Sexualized objects, who care more about how they look than anything else? Or do we become that because we think that's the way for us to be successful?

"I think that the media has one standard that is 'beautiful'—a fair complexion and thin. Yes, it makes me wish that I was thinner and had nicer skin, like the people in magazines and on TV. But I don't get all depressed about it. It's just kind of like it would be really nice to be like that, and maybe someday I will be, but until then I'll have to settle with what I've got. I'm sure there are advantages to being thin and gorgeous. People say that it's not what is on the outside that counts. It's what is on the inside. But practically everyone cares about appearances. I mean, really, say an insanely gorgeous girl walked into a room and on the other side of the room another girl entered who wasn't so beautiful. Who do you think would be noticed first? I don't think it's very hard to figure that out." Maria, 13

"The midriff stereotype affects girls in many ways. I have friends who wear the skimpiest clothes whenever they get the chance, no matter what the weather. The midriff tells girls that if you show off your body, guys will like you. As much as we criticize this effect, it actually works. As much as I think it is wrong, I see my friends changing their style right in front of my face. I am sure it doesn't make them more comfortable, but it's like the old saying: 'sex sells.' I think the midriff does affect me sometimes. It makes me think twice about what I wear. It affects me even more when my friends start dressing like midriffs—then it feels like you have something to prove. Channels like MTV may be manipulative, but they are also smart. All of their techniques seem to work." Jelani, 13

Jelani is a smart, capable student, and an extremely beautiful young woman. She realizes that the way the media manipulates girls is wrong, and sees the midriff archetype for what it is—an advertising tactic that demeans women and makes girls feel bad. At the same time, she feels pressure to fit these painfully impossible stereotypes. Knowing her, I don't think she would be comfortable wearing clothing that flaunts her sexuality shamelessly, yet she admits to feeling some pressure to fit the midriff image.

## Dressing for school

The first time I taught my class, the school I was working in had dress code issues. Summer was coming, and the girls were coming to school in crop tops and super-short skirts. The faculty felt that this was inappropriate clothing for school and wanted to establish a dress code.

The girls were really upset. They felt that the school was taking away their freedom to express themselves. When I talked to them about what kinds of messages they were sending out with their clothes, they understood, and were a little less upset. I told them that while there are occasions for dressing in skimpy clothing, it is important to think about how you are representing yourself with what you wear.

We should certainly feel free to wear what we want, but at the same time we need to be aware of the messages we send with our clothing. Just as you wouldn't wear really sloppy clothes to a fancy dinner, wearing super-revealing clothing is inappropriate for school. I mean, do you really want people to see your cleavage before they see your face?

We should all be sensitive to our own limits and try to notice when the pressure to fit an image dictates what we do, especially if this behavior makes us uncomfortable. We should also try to notice when we judge others based on an unfair standard. If we don't want to be held to this standard, why do we hold our friends to it?

## Messages from the midriff

> She makes girls feel bad about the people they actually are, so much so that they try to become someone else.

> She gives girls an impossible standard by which to judge and criticize themselves and their friends.

> She teaches girls that objectification is okay and that they should in fact be empowered by it.

> She tells us that our looks are the best thing we have going for us, and that we should use them to our advantage as best we can.

> She hurts us because she makes us feel like our appearance is more important than anything else, and if we don't fit the image she represents, we are worth less than she is. She tells us that we should be valued because of what we look like rather than who we are.

Yet we can't seem to get the image out of our heads. The midriff is everywhere! Advertisers love her because the worse she makes us feel about ourselves, the more we will buy their products to improve our looks. We live in a media-saturated world. It's up to us to determine how much these images affect us.

As young women in a society that teaches us to objectify ourselves in order to succeed, we constantly find ourselves under pressure to fit images that don't fit us, to be people that we may not actually want to be. This is the most destructive aspect of the midriff archetype, and the most destructive aspect of the images of women being objectified in the media in general. The midriff style pushes otherwise happy, confident girls to dress and act in ways that are not natural to them. Girls feel bad about the people they actually are, so much so that they try to become someone else. They try to meet an impossible standard, and then use it to judge and criticize themselves and their friends.

## What can you do about it?

I know I have described a HUGE problem, and it seems impossible to do anything about it. To some extent, that's true. Advertisers continue to use images of women acting sexually in order to sell products. While there is certainly increased awareness about the ways these images affect women, I don't think that we can expect to immediately stop seeing spring-break specials featuring girls in wet T-shirt contests and whipped-cream bikinis. I do, however, think that if we can change the way we think about these images, then we can deal with them in a more productive way.

Take a step outside yourself and look at the world through another lens. Try not to think, "I have to be this way because it is what is popular." Instead, try to think about how ridiculous it is that this is what is popular! I realize it's difficult to do this when we feel that people are judging us based on our looks. I understand that no matter what I say in this chapter, you are still going to care about how you look when you leave your house. That's okay, and in fact it's totally normal. It's important to feel good about how we look.

But as I said earlier, there's a big difference between caring about how you look and being obsessed with your appearance. If you are obsessed with how you look and think that your appearance defines you, you devalue the rest of your assets. That, my friends, is the most important message of this chapter. THERE IS SO MUCH MORE TO WHO WE ARE THAN WHAT PEOPLE SEE ON THE OUTSIDE! I think that the best way for us to respond to all of the harmful images of women we see is to remember what makes us who we are, beyond our looks. Remember our reasons to be proud of ourselves.

**Your assignment is...**

**Make a list of ten reasons why you love yourself**. These reasons should have nothing to do with your appearance. They should focus on something deeper: who you are and how you choose to live your life. Think carefully about the reasons you list, and feel free to list more than ten. Consider what makes you a good friend to others, a capable student, a loving family member, a kind pet owner, whatever you want. Keep this list somewhere you will see it all the time.

Take a minute every day to remind yourself that there is more to who you are than the person you see in the mirror. There are thoughts in your head that are meaningful and important, and words that come out of your mouth that are valuable and interesting. There are people who love you for much more than what you look like. Remember that when you die, no one is going to talk about how great you looked on any particular day. People will miss you because of the way you made them laugh or the inspiring things you did for them. Think about it—would you want to be friends with the most beautiful girl in your school, even if she was rude and insensitive? I doubt it.

*** 

**Set a goal for yourself**. Choose a goal that forces you to use more than your looks to achieve it. Try to make this goal one whose fulfilment will make you happy, and will remind you of your personal worth. Mine is that I try to make at least one person smile every day. I have to do something funny or nice to make that happen, and those both require a lot more than killer looks.

"Even the skinniest, prettiest girls probably don't like something about themselves and want to be like someone else. I know it can be hard, but everyone would be so much happier if they realized the GOOD things about themselves, instead of focusing on the not-so-good things."
Thera, 12

Notice the way you represent yourself. The way the media represents women has a huge impact on the way we see ourselves. No doubt. **Pay attention to the language you use to talk about yourself and other women and girls around you**. Use words that strengthen and encourage. It can be empowering to notice and point out someone who is beautiful, but it might feel a bit degrading to use words like 'hot' or 'sexy' even if they seem like compliments. I think you can feel the difference. Pay attention to how you dress and act—are you comfortable in the clothes you are wearing? Do you feel like yourself behaving as you are? It can be really tempting to objectify ourselves when we see images of women being objectified all around us. Try to carry yourself in a way that represents who you really are.

***

**Write in your journal**. What do you think about objectification? Does it affect you? How? Do you think that you can change the way it affects you? I do. It's all a matter of reminding yourself that you have a lot more going for you than just your appearance. That's simply the outside shell that houses all the rest of the good stuff inside you. It's what's inside that makes you the amazing sister, daughter, friend you are. Don't let anyone—especially some advertising executive you've never even met!—tell you otherwise.

"I am waiting for the day when we will
turn our backs on them
and I am waiting
for a celebration of thighs, guts, breasts,
and butts and I am waiting for them
to stop feeding us lies
and I am waiting for the reflection
in mirrors to stop being despised
but to truly be prized
and I am waiting
for everyone to quit censoring
cellulite
and I am waiting for every natural size
to be the perfect size
and I am waiting for the XSs to the XXLs
to unite
and use our voices to be worthy of attention
not our bodies
and I am perpetually waiting for every
shape and every size
to rejoice."                                    Celia, 16

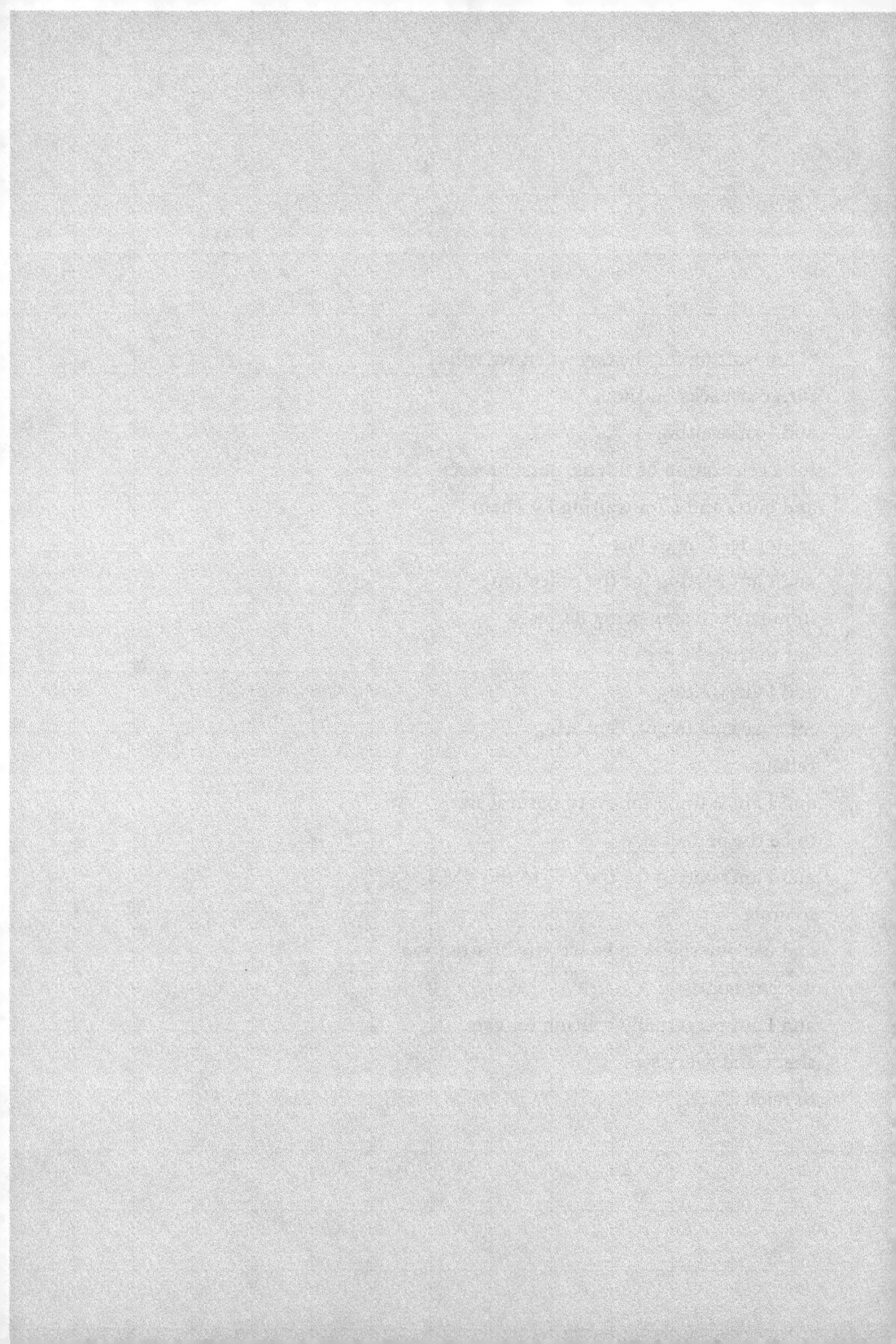

THREE

# How Do I See My Body?

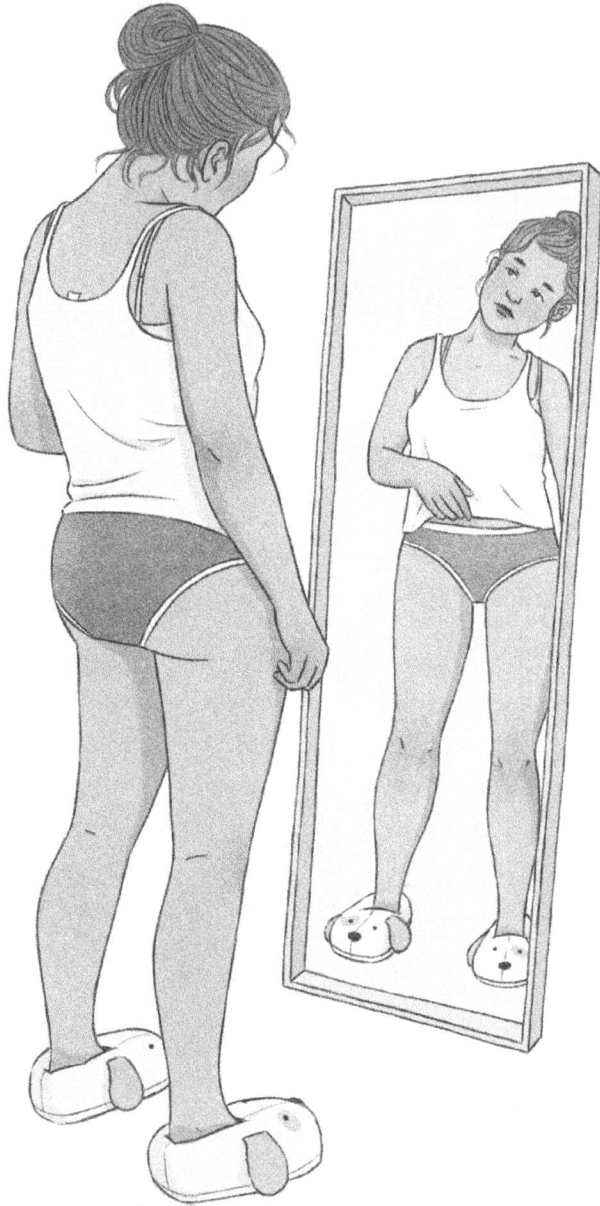

A friend of mine recently confessed to me that she likes to buy magazines like *Cosmopolitan* and *Glamour* when she travels by plane because they're entertaining and easy to read. This friend is a strong, confident woman who generally feels good about herself and her body, even though she doesn't fit the midriff stereotype. She's about five feet nine and probably wears a size 12 or 14. She isn't overly obsessed with her looks, beyond making sure that she looks presentable. Even so, she said, every time she reads the magazines, she ends up feeling bad about herself. She compares herself to the photographs and wishes her body were different. She knows that these magazines are ridiculous, and that the images in them are not realistic for her body. You can feel great about yourself and be confident, she told me, but these photographs still infect your brain.

I agree with her, and I'll explain why. I have a good self-image, particularly about my body. I strive to be proud of my accomplishments, and consider my body to be one of them. I have never been skinny and was always heavier than I wanted to be in high school. I tried tons of diets and exercise programs; nothing worked. I just couldn't get rid of that extra layer of fat. By changing my eating habits and working out, I've changed my body. For a while, I was taking dance classes five days a week, and can now jump higher and balance better than ever before. I'm more flexible and can do dance moves that seemed impossible a year ago. I'm proud of the way I've developed my body, and feel comfortable standing in front of a mirror in a leotard and tights in a room full of other women who are definitely thinner than I am. I wear a size 10 or 12; most of my dancing peers probably wear a 4 or 6, or even a 2 or a 0. I've worked very hard to get to where I am, both physically and emotionally, and feel good about myself when I look in that mirror. I am still not—nor will I ever be—'skinny,' but I can definitely walk into class and feel fine about my body.

But still, every time I see women with that 'ideal body'—on TV, online, in real life—a part of me wishes I had that model body. I can't help but feel inadequate, even though I know my body is beautiful and capable of incredible things. I struggle to love my body completely. I can't stand the fact that there are sneaking thoughts in my brain that make me second-guess my love for myself. I am upset that I can't totally control the way that I feel about my appearance.

**How does the world see me?**

Developing a healthy image of our bodies is one of the biggest challenges facing women and girls today. No matter how beautiful we are, we can easily find something to criticize. There are always a few pounds we could lose, or a muscle group that could be more toned. And it's not just women who are challenged by the way they feel about their bodies. I know plenty of men who struggle with their body image, and wish they looked different.

But this problem tends to be more challenging for women for two reasons, both of which relate to our discussion in the last chapter. First of all, we live in a society that too often values us for the way we look rather than who we are. This encourages us to make our appearance more important than anything else, and to obsess about it. Second, the representations of feminine beauty that society applauds are unrealistic for most of us. I know that no matter how much I exercise or how much salad I eat, I will never look like the women I see in the media.

## The scoop on eating[1]

> Your body is changing. It's important to eat nutritious food to feel energetic.

> It's not uncommon for both girls and guys to be concerned with weight and food. But don't let the scale run your life. The numbers on the scale don't reflect your self worth.

> TV and magazines have bizarre ideas of what people should look like. Don't believe that this is what you should look like.

> How you feel can affect what you eat. For example, some people may not eat if they feel stressed out. Others may eat when they are bored or depressed. This is called 'emotional eating.'

> What you eat can also affect how you feel. Healthy, nutritious food will give you energy and make you feel strong and alive. Sugar and junk food will make you feel down and cloudy.

### Diet—a definition

> The usual food and drink of a person or animal.

> A regulated selection of foods, as for medical reasons or cosmetic weight loss.

So your diet is simply what you eat. But we've come to think of the second definition—a regulated selection of foods—when we say the word diet. The diet industry, which includes books and plans and special foods and gimmicks to lose weight, thrives on the fact that we don't feel so good about our bodies. Americans spend over $40 million a year on diet-related products.[2]

"I think that body image is a very big thing in the lives of people, especially teenagers. I think that it affects me a lot because sometimes—actually a lot of times—I think that I look fat. Other people who are skinny and say that they are fat make me feel morbidly obese. I think that when the whole world looks at me, they see 'the fat girl.'

"Growing up in this generation where hip-hop and rap are very popular, it's hard for me to feel as good as I should about myself. All of the skinny girls that are on videos make me feel fat. I always wish that I could have a body like the girls on the videos. It makes me very mad at myself. I wish people could live instead of constantly getting judged. I guess life just isn't that easy." Makhala, 13

I can't help but notice that right before Makhala says that she wishes people didn't have to constantly be judged, she judges herself! Twice—first she judges her body, wishing it were like the girls in the videos, then she judges her attitude about her body. She's angry at herself for wishing she were thinner. I am not criticizing her for feeling the way she does, I am just pointing out how easily we criticize ourselves, and how hard we make it to be proud of ourselves and how we look.

## The pressure to be thin

Remember what we learned from the midriff? "Your body is your best asset. Flaunt your sexuality, even if you don't understand it." For girls who aren't completely confident about their bodies—which I would guess is most of us—this message has a second layer. If our bodies are our best assets and are not what we want them to be, we think less of ourselves. "Do I look fat in this?" is probably the most often-heard question in women's dressing rooms. This pressure has different impacts on people, and manifests itself in different ways. Girls everywhere are dieting and engaging in behavior that is destructive to their bodies. A national health study found that 40 percent of nine- and ten-year-old girls reported that they were trying to lose weight.[3] That's almost half of nine- and ten-year-old girls! That's insane. And that's the society in which we live.

## Eating right

Everyone needs to eat to live. It's important to remember that our bodies are the external representations of who we are, and we want those bodies to be healthy. One of the most important aspects of being healthy is eating right, to feed our bodies and our minds.

Develop healthy eating habits:

> Eat breakfast. It gets your metabolism going for the day.

> Don't skip meals. This will lead to overeating at later meals.

> Eat fruits and vegetables. Eating fruits and vegetables three to five times a day decreases all kinds of health risks, including cancer, heart attacks, strokes, and obesity.

> Eat plenty of iron. Teenage girls who are menstruating (having their periods) are at risk of anemia, which is a deficiency of iron. You can get iron from broccoli, potatoes, kidney beans, red meat, eggs, and whole grains.

> Drink water. Eight glasses a day is ideal. Our bodies are more than 60 percent water, so we need to keep them well supplied with fresh water all the time!

Eat a variety of foods every day, balancing between the following:

> Vegetables. Eat at least three to five servings per day. Eat a variety of vegetables—different vegetables have different nutrients in them. The tastiest vegetables are those that are in season where you live. They didn't have to travel far to get to your table.

> Fruits. Eat at least two to four servings per day. If you can, eat fresh, locally grown fruits. They are tastier and better for the environment.

> Carbohydrates (bread, rice, pasta). These will fill you up easily but don't have all the nutrients you need. Be sure to balance them with fruits, vegetables, etc.

> Dairy (milk, yogurt, cheese). Three or more servings per day.

> Protein (meat, poultry, fish, beans, eggs, nuts). Two to three servings per day.

Avoid processed foods that are simply unhealthy. Stay away from things like chips, candy or any food with ingredients you can't pronounce or don't recognize.

Take a minute to notice what you eat every day. So many teenagers eat mostly processed foods. These foods are bad for you (don't really give you any nutrients and usually just rot your teeth and insides), and they are bad for the environment (lots of energy is wasted to create them, package them, and ship them).

**Taking it too far**

For some of us, the pressure to be thin is kind of in the back of our minds, and it pops up every once in a while. For others, it is there most of the time, reminding them that they are not who they want to be because they don't look as good as they would like. For others still, the pressure to be thin overwhelms their lives, and dictates how they act all the time.

When I was fourteen years old, I went to summer camp (like I did every summer) with my friends. We hung out, gossiped, flirted with boys, went swimming and camping—all the regular things you would expect a bunch of adolescent girls to do at camp. It was a pretty normal summer for us, like the ones before it. And it was great. I mean, it was camp—it was perfect. Our main responsibility was to have fun with our friends.

Except for one thing—my friends and I started to notice that our friend Samantha had pretty much stopped eating. She was looking awfully skinny, and at meals we would watch her avoid everything but a few carrots. It was starting to get scary, because we could see the bones in her cheeks and neck. Her face had sort of sunken in, and it looked like her skin was hanging off her bones. She was really starting to look sick. We didn't know what to do. Should we say something to her? Would she get mad at us? Should we tell our counselor?

As the days went by, Samantha looked sicker and sicker. Not only was she not eating, but we thought we heard her throwing up after lunch one day. That was when we realized this was serious. Our friend was hurting herself, and we were watching it happen. I wanted to help her, but I didn't know how. I was afraid to say anything to her because I didn't want to upset her. Samantha was one of my best friends. But I knew that I had to try to help her. Luckily, I felt close enough to my parents to talk to them about what was happening. My dad is a psychologist, and I thought he might have some good advice.

I talked to my parents when they came up to camp for visiting day, and another friend of mine talked to hers. Together, we all decided that we had to talk to Samantha's parents and let them know what we had been seeing all summer. I was nervous. All the parents had a big talk while we waited to hear what was going to happen.

At the end of the talk, Samantha and her parents went off on their own, and my dad told me that Samantha's parents were going to talk to the nurse, who would be monitoring her weight for the rest of the summer. If she lost any more weight, he told me, she would have to go home. I definitely did not want my friend sent home from camp. I felt awful.

Luckily, the thought of having to leave camp motivated Samantha to start eating, at least enough so that she could stay. I honestly don't know how she did it, because I don't remember her eating much, even after the visiting day talk. But somehow she managed to stay at camp. I was glad. When she got home, Samantha started seeing a psychologist, who helped her deal with the issues she was facing. She has since gotten her eating problem under control. I don't think she has such a bad relationship with food anymore.

I have a number of friends besides Samantha who have experienced eating disorders. Off the top of my head, I can think of five, including one person who was so ill that she had to go to a treatment center. She lived there so that the doctors could monitor her weight, and watch how many calories she was taking in. She almost died from starving herself. Luckily, she survived, and is now a lot healthier. But, like almost everyone I know who has suffered from an eating disorder, her relationship with food may challenge her for many years.

### What is an eating disorder?

Let's take a second to get the facts straight. Eating disorders involve having an unhealthy relationship with food. Some people severely cut down the number of calories they eat, or even stop eating altogether, like Samantha tried to do. These people suffer from anorexia (they're anorexic). Some people binge and purge—eat a lot and then force themselves to throw up, take laxatives, or exercise compulsively to get rid of the calories they've taken in. They suffer from bulimia (they're bulimic).

"It's a control thing—if you choose not to eat, you can control something. I don't think I will ever be at the point that I was—I am much more confident about myself and who I am, and it's not that important to be skinny.

"My grandma was always a person who told me I needed to be skinny and watch what I ate. As a kid, I felt like if I were to reach for that extra cookie, they would all be watching me. When I was in high school I would eat a roll of Life Savers™ a day. And that was it.

"It started with Slim-Fast™. You are supposed to eat two shakes a day, a piece of fruit, and then a healthy dinner. I cut the shakes first, because they weren't good and seemed like a waste of calories. Then I cut the healthy dinner. I was just down to the piece of fruit. Then I cut the fruit and I would just drink water. And the Life Savers™. They had calories, but no fat.

"I would get up every morning at five or six to do a workout video before school. During gym, I would go on the treadmill in the weight room because the treadmill tells you how many calories you are burning. I was always trying to see how many calories I could burn in one period. I slowly convinced myself that I didn't like certain foods, until I didn't like anything anymore.

"My eating disorder started when I was sixteen, but I was on diets starting in sixth grade. And my parents encouraged it. Not that they wanted me to have an eating disorder, but they encouraged me to be thin. I would convince myself that I ate. And I really believed I had [eaten]. That was the most destructive part of the whole thing.

"Even when you don't eat, your weight goes up and down. The lowest I ever got was 125 pounds, but I was friends with people who weighed 104. I didn't understand why I couldn't get that thin." Jenny, 27

Although Jenny eats normally now, she says that food will always be an issue for her. Eating disorders are mental disorders. Not everyone is susceptible to them, and some people are more likely than others to have them. People who develop eating disorders usually have other issues they

## Some common eating disorders[4]

### > Anorexia Nervosa

**What Is It**: A person does not eat enough because of a strong fear of becoming fat. People with anorexia get thinner and thinner, sometimes starving themselves to death.

**Common Signs and Symptoms**: Skipping meals and/or eating very little, feeling cold all the time, believing that you are fat in spite of being thin, wearing lots of baggy clothes to hide weight loss

### > Bulimia Nervosa

**What Is It**: A person eats a large amount of food (binges) and then gets rid of it (purges). People with bulimia fear weight gain, but they usually stay at a normal weight or are slightly overweight.

**Common Signs and Symptoms**: Eating a large amount of food in a short period of time, purposely causing yourself to vomit, using laxatives, or exercising excessively, having feelings of shame, guilt, and being out of control

### > Binge Eating

**What Is It**: A person eats a large amount of food in a short period of time without purging. Binge eaters often dislike themselves for getting fat, but can't stop overeating. This may lead to heart attacks, diabetes, or circulation problems.

**Common Signs and Symptoms**: Eating a large amount of food in a short period of time, having feelings of shame, guilt, and being out of control, gaining weight, eating when depressed or anxious

are dealing with, often about control in their lives. Eating disorders don't really go away, but with help, people can find a way to have a healthy relationship with food. Treatment usually involves therapy, and sometimes medication. People who develop eating disorders are often dealing with a number of issues, like depression, low self-esteem, dysfunctional family dynamics, history of sexual or physical abuse, or other psychological problems. These factors are important to consider when people are treated for eating disorders. But the cultural part of this issue—how people strive to meet an unrealistic standard of beauty—cannot be ignored.

Many women don't fit neatly into the categories of anorexia or bulimia, but fall somewhere on a spectrum of eating-disordered behaviors. In fact, one of the medical criteria used to diagnose anorexia is having a body weight that is 15 percent below what is considered 'normal.' This would apply to the majority of models. The pressure to be thin affects women more than men to an overwhelming degree—ten times more women than men suffer from eating disorders.[5] We all do things to ourselves that reflect the negative image we have of our bodies. I would guess that every female friend of mine has been on some sort of diet at one point or another in her life. Lots of women have taken diet pills and/ or laxatives, exercised compulsively, or done something else to their bodies to try to change them.

I don't want you to worry that you will develop an eating disorder if you continue to be self-conscious about your body. I don't want to scare you or make you nervous. There is a big difference between being self-conscious and having an eating disorder. But I do want to make you aware of the connection between how we see ourselves and how we treat ourselves. Most women and girls I know have a hard time seeing their bodies in a positive light, especially during adolescence. It is very easy to dislike our bodies when we constantly see photographs of models that make us feel self-conscious.

### Getting help

If you have a friend who you think might have an eating disorder, or if you think you might have one yourself, get help. Talk to an adult you trust. This person can help you or your friend find a professional who can help begin the healing process. You can also take a first step by calling the National Eating Disorders Hotline at (800) 931-2237.

The behavior patterns that lead to eating disorders are directly connected to the messages our society gives us about our bodies, and the way we take in those messages. Criticizing ourselves because of how we feel about how we look, puts us at risk of doing destructive things to ourselves. For some of us, our obsession with our bodies is not such a big problem; we deal with it and go on with our lives. For others, this obsession can physically hurt us, or maybe even kill us. No matter how you slice it, this is no laughing matter. Our society tells us to be thin, and we hurt ourselves trying to get there. Something has to change.

**What can you do about it?**

Here again we have another problem that seems impossible to solve. As I said in the previous chapter, I don't think the images we see of women—the impossible standards by which we judge our appearances—will go away quickly. However, I do think that we can take our relationships with our bodies into our own hands. While we can't completely control the social standard set for us, we can control the way we see ourselves within the context of that standard.

I am more confident about my body than I ever have been in my life. I can say without hesitation that I feel great about the way that I look. While there are always things I can say that I want to improve about my appearance, I am finally at a point where I can say that I love the way I look, and feel good about what I see when I look in the mirror, even when I am naked.

It has taken me a long time to get to this point. Only in the past few years have I been able to say these things about my appearance with real confidence. I have worked very hard—both physically and emotionally—to get where I am today. I am proud of myself and of what I have achieved.

I am proud of the way I look. My body represents many hours in the dance studio, and a great deal of diligence and discipline. I am also proud of the way I feel about how I look. That achievement represents the fact that I recognize that I am who I am, and I have the body I do, one that will never be like the ones I see on TV or in ads. But I still love the way I look, despite the millions of influences telling me I should feel otherwise.

Don't get me wrong. I don't feel this way every second of every day, but even when I doubt myself, I can remember feeling proud of how I look, and I can find my way back to that feeling.

I want you to be able to feel equally good about your body. I can't promise that this will happen right away. I can say, though, that if you commit yourself to making this change, you will be able to get there too.

**Your assignment is...**

First of all, I recommend that you **do some kind of physical activity** as often as possible, at least four times a week. Make your workouts fun, so you can look forward to them—work out with a friend, or listen to music while you exercise, or play a sport you like. Working out gets the blood pumping through your veins, and gets your heart running. These things naturally make people feel better—less tired, less lethargic, more energized. Those are all good things that will contribute to an improved sense of self.

Also, as you work out, you will start to see results, but it is important not to be looking for specific results right away. Doing crunches every day will not necessarily make your stomach flat (I've tried), and push-ups aren't going to automatically give you toned arms (I've tried that too). Instead, come up with a workout plan for yourself that combines cardio activity (stuff that gets your heart rate up) with muscle toning and stretching. Make yourself a schedule and stick to it. Set short-term goals that are reasonable to achieve. As you achieve these goals, set new goals, ones that are harder. Be proud of all of your accomplishments, and remember to smile every time you look in the mirror. I am emotionally empowered because I am physically strong; you can achieve the same thing.

Working out is the easy part. It's a lot harder to change the way you think about yourself, but this is where the real work begins. The best thing you can do for yourself is to **think positively about your body image**. Every day, affirm something about yourself. When you look in the mirror, compliment your body in some way. Remember to think about all the things you wouldn't be able to do if you didn't have your body. Every time you look at your thighs and dislike them, think about the fact that you wouldn't be able to walk, run or jump if your thighs weren't as strong as they are. Next time you criticize your wide hips, remind yourself that you won't be able to have a baby if you don't have wide hips. The hips might not be something you need right now, but having them is part of what makes you a strong, beautiful woman.

\*\*\*

**Be a model of self-esteem for others**. Being around self-conscious people makes us self-conscious. Try to avoid putting yourself in situations in which everyone is putting themselves down. I know what these scenes are like—it becomes cool to talk negatively about yourself, and you seem like an egomaniacal freak if you think highly of yourself. "I am so fat today! I ate three M&Ms!" Try to turn those situations around if you can. Emphasize the great yoga class you went to and encourage your friends to come. Invite your friends over to eat a good, healthy meal together. Help yourself and your friends feel GOOD about your bodies. If you can do this, it will help you, and the women around you.

***

**Pay attention to the language you use to talk about yourself**. It's in our hands to change the way we talk about ourselves. There is a huge difference between saying, "Hmmm...I am out of shape. I want to start to work out more," or "I've been eating a lot of junk food lately. I want to eat healthier food," and "I am SO BAD! I ate a whole cookie today!" or "I look so fat in this dress!" I may feel unsatisfied with what I see in the mirror, but my response can be denigrating or empowering. I can dislike myself, or I can take action.

***

**Like your look!** Wear clothes that you are comfortable in, not ones that make you more self-conscious. Try to choose things to wear that are flattering to your body—no matter how cute something looks on the hanger, if you don't like how it looks on you, you won't like wearing it. It's no fun to wear an outfit that you don't like, even if it is the most stylish thing out there.

"Giving someone a compliment a day might help more than you think. Some girls just dress a certain way for attention, so if they got a simple compliment, that might help them, and fulfill the want for attention."

**Alanah, 13**

**Compliment the people around you** to create a more positive tone. Giving compliments makes people feel better, and will help you feel good too. Try to create an environment for you and your friends in which it is comfortable to think highly of oneself and have high self-esteem. Try, as often as possible, to be around people who make you feel good about yourself. If your friends don't make you feel good, think about hanging out with some new people, ones who won't damage your self-image.

\*\*\*

**Write in your journal**. Use it as a place to vent when you feel down. Use it as a way to record your accomplishments, and to remind yourself to be proud of what you've achieved. Feeling good about your body is not easy, considering all of the external pressures we experience and all of the negative messages we receive. Combating these messages is something we have to do from within ourselves and inside our circles of friends. We aren't going to completely change the messages out there, but we can definitely change the way they affect us.

\*\*\*

Most importantly, **honor your body**. My body is the physical expression of myself. It is my home, the container for my soul. My body is magic—the way everything functions is really miraculous. My body knows how to turn food into energy, to maintain my heartbeat and to do many other things that make it possible for me to live. As a woman, my body can carry and birth life. So, as I see it, my body has magic in it. I honor this magic and I honor my body. And I expect others to do the same. Tell yourself, every day, out loud: "My body is magic. I honor my body and expect the same respect from others." Remember, only you can make decisions about what happens to your body. Make choices that come from your understanding of the magic you carry, which reminds you to honor yourself and your body.

"I just want to say that I feel the most beautiful and perfect people are the ones who are internally happy, and don't judge themselves by other people's standards. I was always taught that it's not what is on the outside that matters, it's what's within. It's your turn to learn that lesson." Jelani, 13

**A word about our cycles**

The cycles that happen in our bodies are sacred and are the source of all life. Yet, our culture has taught us that menstruation is a taboo subject, something to be kept secret, in a dark corner of ourselves. Sometimes we hear messages which teach us that menstruation is dirty, and that we are impure when we are bleeding. This is a great misunderstanding. There is tremendous power in this cycle and particularly in the time of bleeding. If we really listen to our bodies, we can learn secrets from our wombs and gain new perspectives about our dreams and visions. Menstruation is not dirty, and explaining why our culture sees it as such would require a whole book. I will simply say this:

It is a great gift to be a woman. I am proud to be a woman. Part of being a woman means menstruating. This can sometimes be uncomfortable or messy, but if I understand how to relate to this cycle then I can connect to the power within it. I can understand that the blood that comes from my womb is my body's way of releasing what it does not need—just as it does when I pee or when I forget a memory that doesn't serve me anymore. This release allows for the birth of something new inside my body and inside myself. This subject is so deep that it would also take a whole book to really get into it. There is a lifetime of learning available to us if we really pay attention to our cycle and to the messages our wombs are sending us. Notice—in the days after we finish bleeding, we can do the work of four women because we have a burst of energy rushing through us. When we are bleeding, we are often sluggish and tired because our body is working hard to release and needs us to rest and relax. We might be more irritable during this time (or before, as your body is getting ready to bleed) because what we really want is to be quiet and to be alone. Give yourself time to rest when you are bleeding. Eat warm food that is nourishing. Keep in mind that during your period, you and your body are in a different state from the rest of your cycle and you have different needs. Try to listen to your body to hear what those needs are and fulfill them.

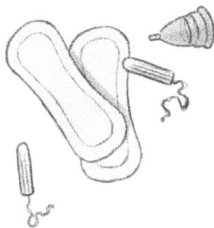

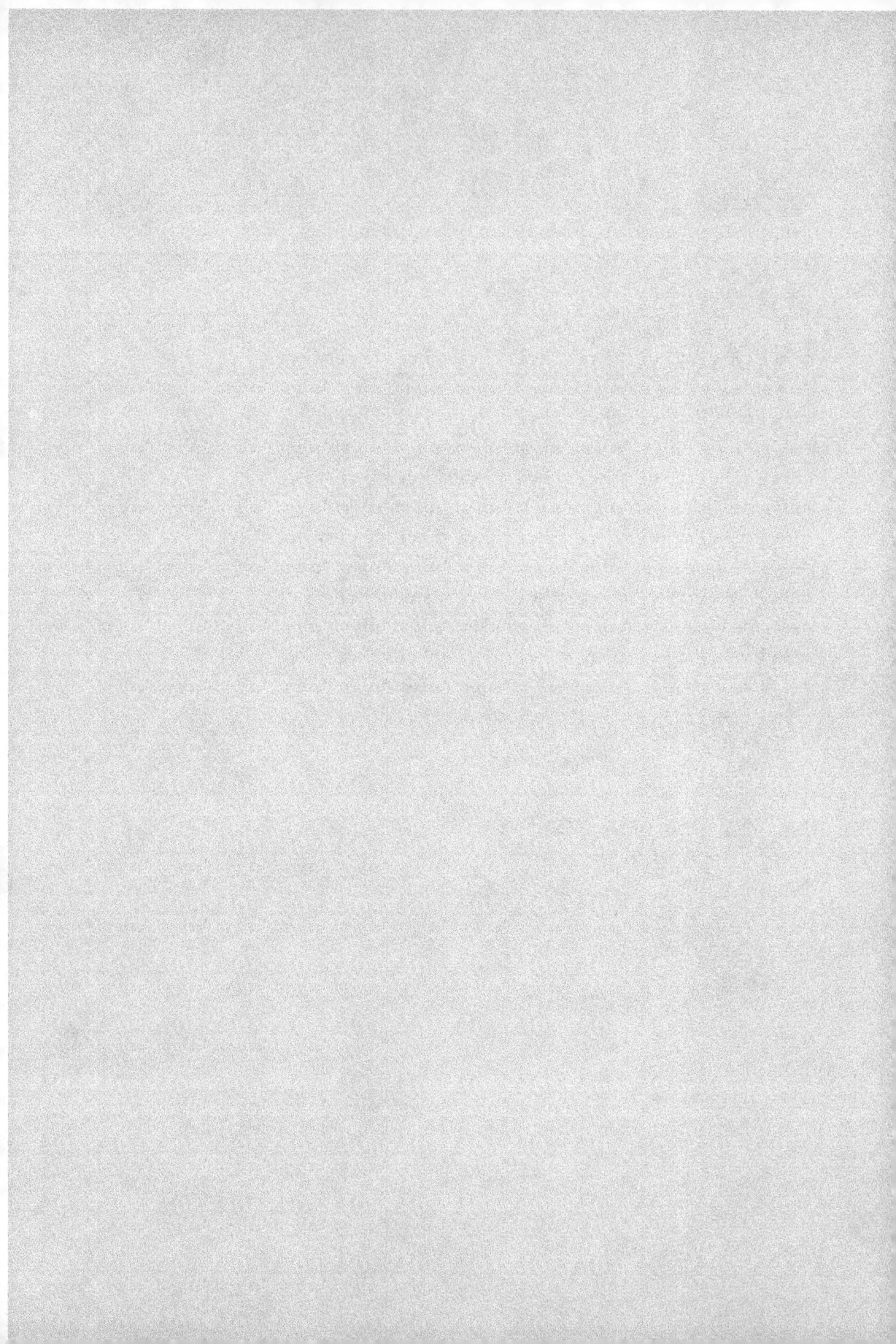

FOUR

# Friends or Enemies?

I went to a small school from kindergarten through eighth grade, and had only 23 kids in my grade in middle school. Almost all of us had known each other since kindergarten. Most people were friendly, but there were definitely cliques, and there was one clearly popular clique.

I was in the popular clique, but I wasn't the most popular girl in our grade. I cared a lot about membership in the popular clique, and didn't want to lose it for anything. I let my 'friends' make fun of me a lot, and got really upset when they treated me badly. I never did anything about it, though. It was awful.

### Popular—a definition

> Widely liked or appreciated; a popular resort.

> Liked by acquaintances; sought after for company.

"A lot of girls think about cliques and the 'cool group.' Girls start to ask themselves, 'Do guys like me? Am I considered a cool person?' If they see that another person is getting what they want, they'll want to be like that person. Usually that person is acting mean, so then girls try to be mean, just to belong. Girls act mean in front of their friends, but when the group is not around, they can act the way they want. Girls just act mean in front of their friends to show off." Emily, 14

Amongst our friends, we weren't exactly nice to each other. The stronger girls in the group bullied each other, not in the give-me-your-money kind of way, more in the listen-to-me-and-do-what-I-say-or-else kind of way. We were best friends and worst enemies.

For a few summers at camp, I was in a pretty obnoxious clique. Only now do I really realize how horrible we actually were. I can't tell you how many people have told me as adults that they couldn't stand me when they first met me. I understand why. I was overweight and insecure, and as a result I was mean to most of the people around me. And I had a big mouth, so I would pretty much say whatever I wanted to other kids, to counselors, to teachers, to my parents. I definitely did not think about how my words affected other people.

"I think that when girls are mean to each other, they mainly do it because someone else has been mean to them. I think it's like a circle—it goes around and around. We also are mean to each other because we judge people so much. We end up making fun of people because of the clothes they wear, or how they look.

"I don't think that we will ever be all the way perfect, but I do think we can try. To try, I think we should start by forgiving people for old mistakes. Then we should try to look at people on the inside, not the outside. That is very important.

"Everybody has been mean to people before, so we all know how it feels. It feels like that person hates you. Even if it's something small, it hurts you like it is the biggest insult somebody could say to you. It is not a good thing, and we should try to stop it altogether." Makhala, 13

Inside our clique, one of my 'friends' really terrorized me. She was cruel. Almost anything I did provoked a mean response. The other girls just followed her because they were afraid she'd turn on them too. I wasn't as much of a follower; I told her if I was pissed off about something she had done. But when I did, she'd be rude and embarrass me in front of other people. I know that I am not the only woman who has stories of girls treating her badly as an adolescent. Unfortunately, this behavior is a rite of passage for lots of teenage girls.

In every class I've taught, all my students can relate to the discussion about meanness and competition. Everyone has been both a victim and a perpetrator. We've all been mean to other people, even though we have also experienced meanness ourselves, and know how much it hurts.

### Are girls meaner than boys?

Girls can be more ruthless than boys. When boys are angry with each other, they tend to fight—sometimes physically—and once their disagreement is over, they forget whatever it was that upset them. While this isn't always the case, it's true in general. Girls, on the other hand, tend to be far less direct. They'll talk about people behind their backs, or—this is a big one—purposefully exclude people from their plans. Without ever actually saying so, we let other girls know that they don't fit in, and they're not welcome to hang out with us.

"Girls are just as aggressive as boys, just in different ways. Boys are physically aggressive, while girls mentally hurt each other. I think that girls do this because they are smarter than boys when it comes to this kind of stuff." Jennie, 14

"Boys are known to be very aggressive and mean toward each other, but people don't realize that girls are also mean to each other. They are not as mean in a physical way, but they can mentally abuse one another. A lot of girls are mean and try to hurt each other because they are jealous. Some girls will be completely rude and mean if they are jealous of you. Or in other cases, if they are jealous of you, they will try to befriend you. Girls will sometimes do anything to be 'the best.'" Amanda, 13

### What does meanness look like?

I can't tell you how many terrible stories I've heard. In one of my classes, we read an article about meanness that included a story about one girl calling another to ask her opinion about a third girl. The girl they were talking about had been secretly conferenced in, and heard everything that was said about her. When we talked about the article the next day, I brought up the story as a can-you-believe-how-ridiculous-this-is type of thing, and my students told me that it really happens, all the time. I was shocked.

Then I remembered what it had been like for me, how it felt to be an adolescent girl. I reminded myself that it really is that difficult. Girls can really be that mean. I remembered my own adolescence, and thought about tons of so-called friends of mine who pushed me around. I remembered being left out of people's plans. I remembered the rumors about me flying around behind my back. I remembered that being an adolescent girl meant living in a completely crazy world.

## Another world

The rules in girl world are unique. There are certain standards by which everyone judges everyone else, and if you don't meet these standards (no one really does), you get made fun of and left out. The standards girls use to judge each other are different, depending on who makes the rules in your world.

In most schools, there are some leaders—the girls who are the most popular, who sort of get to tell everyone else what to do. They decide what the style is, and set the trends for how people should dress. They get first dibs on the boys, and decide who gets to go out with whom. They decide who is popular, and who is allowed to hang out with them. These leader girls hold lots of power.

It's easy to identify these girls. They are the ones who usually look like they are dressed for a fashion show rather than for school, and have at least a few other girls with them at all times. These girls are their sidekicks. They follow the leader around, and do whatever she says. The leader likes having them around because they tend not to question what she says, often because they are too afraid of her. The sidekicks' popularity depends (in their minds, at least) on remaining friends with the leader. (Flip back to Chapter One, where Rosalind Wiseman characterizes girls' roles in cliques.)

These kinds of friend groupings are recipes for disaster. On one hand, you have the leader, who tells the other girls how to act. She knows how powerful she is, and uses her power to get her way all the time. This isn't healthy for her, because she learns that being obnoxious will help her get her way, which isn't really true outside of girl world. In the rest of the world, this girl wouldn't get much respect. On the other hand, you have the followers, the girls who do whatever the leader says. These girls learn that thinking for yourself and questioning authority are bad, and will only get you in trouble. I don't really think this makes for meaningful friendships.

Now, I realize that the girls I described above look like pretty exaggerated caricatures of people. But girls like that really do exist, everywhere. Their behavior is that ridiculous. It's strange how it happens. I mean, inside, both of these types of girls are probably perfectly nice people with minds of their own, capable of making good decisions, but they don't get the chance to show that side of themselves because they are trapped in girl world and can't see out.

"In a lot of schools, girls try to be the same, wear the same clothes, or their hair the same way. For example, some girls will make 'rules' for being 'cool.' Like you can only wear jeans on Tuesday, and your hair up in a ponytail once a week, ridiculous things like that."

**Jennie, 14**

This is not to say that these are the only types of girls there are, and that we all fit into one of those two narrow categories. Certainly, even the nastiest leaders have moments when they do nice things for other people. And the blindest followers actually do have minds of their own that they use every once in a while. The characters I've described represent types of behavior we see in ourselves and the people around us. The leader/follower dynamic is one of many behaviors that become exaggerated among adolescent girls.

## Extreme behavior

Part of the package that comes with being an adolescent girl is exaggerated behavior, and extreme hostility is only one kind of exaggerated behavior, though it may be the worst. There were times when I was an adolescent that I acted so crazy I didn't even recognize myself. I would get really emotional about things, especially when I was upset. I would fight with my parents, and get so angry that I'd forget why we originally started the fight. I would yell and scream and just be altogether obnoxious. I would get equally mad at my friends when they were mean, but I usually contained my anger more because I knew I could lose my friends. But no matter how awful I was to my family, they would still be there for me. So I vented.

My friends and I did not hesitate to use whatever we could against each other. We were always competing with one another, and did whatever we could to keep the others down.

Intense competition is another behavior that gets really exaggerated among adolescent girls, and is often what sparks meanness. It's almost as if there is only so much coolness to go around, and we are fighting to hold on to as much of it as we can. The more we have, the more we fit in. If we are cool enough, we control what it means to fit in. (Or at least we act like we do. I still think the media largely tells us what is cool.)

## Girl against girl

One reason competition among girls gets so intense is because, generally more so than men and boys, women and girls are very aware of social hierarchies, or the social structures in which we live.

We understand that there are some people who are leaders and some who are not. We know who has power and who influences others. We also know who we need to befriend if we want to change our own social status. We are also very skilled at hurting other people, especially our friends.

"While it would be wrong to say that all boys or all girls deal with situations a certain way, it can certainly be generalized that boys and girls react to situations differently. When boys get angry, they confront each other and often physically fight. Girls, on the other hand, do not say anything to each other's faces, but rather spread rumors behind each other's backs, or turn people against each other. We deal with situations in backstabbing, mentally exhausting ways. It is one of the hardest parts of growing up being a teenage girl. Considering all the pressure and abuse we receive from the media and boys, why is it that we join in and torture each other?

"The movie *Mean Girls* shows it all. Cady, a sweet, timid girl, moves from Africa to the United States, and for the first time in her life goes to a regular suburban high school. The movie details her crossover into the world of bitchy teenage girls. After about a month in her new school, she is tricking one of her friends into eating 'weight loss' bars that actually make the girl gain weight. She turns her friends against each other through secrets and gossip, and steals someone's boyfriend. While the characters in the movie show extreme cases of bitchy girl behavior, in reality, many girls act very similarly to those in the movie.

"I don't know any girls who have never spread a rumor about someone, or never talked behind another girl's back. While it seems that most girls realize this is mean and hurtful behavior, we still participate in it. The strangest part is that the plans that girls develop to hurt each other are very intelligent and well thought out. We know exactly who to talk to, what to say, what buttons to push; we know how to psychologically break each other. So while many people think teenage girls are unintelligent, shopping-obsessed idiots, the truth is that we are just channeling our intelligence in the wrong direction." Amy, 15

Amy sums it all up really well. I especially appreciate her point about how we are channeling our intelligence. The way girls treat each other demonstrates how smart we actually are in social situations. As Amy said, we know what to do and say to really hurt each other. And because, as adolescents, we sometimes find ourselves in a world in which there is no compassion, we pull out all the stops when we need to. We can be horribly cruel in sneaky ways. This kind of meanness really hurts, but even though we all know how it feels to be on the receiving end of it, we do it anyway. WHY!?!?

**Being mean to feel better**

I've explained that we understand the complexities of social situations, and we know how to work within them to try to improve our own status. But I don't think that explains why girls treat people they call their best friends like dirt. There is more to it than that.

112

"Many girls today aren't the nicest people. They gossip, spread rumors, make fun of people, and more. You may think you don't do any of these things, but I bet that almost everyone in the entire world has gossiped or made fun of someone, even if it was in nursery school. Luckily, our school (hopefully) is not one of the schools that has kids crying because of what someone did to them. I feel terrible for the kids who have to go through that every day of their school years. But the girls aren't nasty for their own health; they do it to be more popular or cool. Sometimes during a girl's teenage years she starts to feel bad about herself. She makes fun of other people so that she feels better about herself and makes the others look worse. It's not fair, but it's true.

"It's a shame that girls don't know another way to feel better about themselves. Hopefully in the future 'mean girls' will see how unfair and selfish they are, and find another way to help themselves." Ali, 12

Ali's point is really well taken: sometimes we are mean to each other in order to feel better about ourselves. Our insecurity overwhelms us, and as a result we look at other people to see what we can criticize. If we can make them feel bad about something, we can feel a little bit better ourselves.

Remember what Jelani said in Chapter One: "I have hurt people by talking about them. I guess it's like the more flaws I uncover about someone else, the more perfect I am. When I say things to people in front of their faces, it helps me break them down into how little and insignificant I want them to be."

Wow. Sad but true. If we feel bad about ourselves, one of the easiest ways for us to deal with that is to make other people feel worse. But actually this makes the problem worse. By being mean, we contribute to a climate of nastiness that hurts us as well as the people around us. The more we perpetuate cruel behavior, the more we should expect to be treated badly ourselves. So in our effort to feel better about ourselves, we actually end up making ourselves feel worse; eventually someone will point out our flaws, just like we pointed out hers.

"The idea of mean girls is not something new to me. At my school, I personally have experienced some really mean behavior. Today I know that I am not part of the 'popular' clique, and I am okay with that. I have my friends, and am 100 percent happy, but last year it was much harder.

"For some reason, it was very important for me to be in the 'popular' clique. I was in a tough position in my life. I felt my family deemed me inadequate. I was looking for approval in all aspects of my life. I became exactly what my parents wanted of me, even if doing so gave up some of my true personality.

"I saw in the TV shows and movies that the beautiful, popular girls were always happy, and everyone liked them or wanted to be them. I felt that the key to happiness was to be part of the 'popular' clique in our school. I started trying to be friends with this clique, but it backfired. Some days I would think to myself, 'Hey, I think they're starting to like me,' and the next day, when they completely excluded me, purposely, from their plans, I would think that I was inadequate, that something was wrong with me.

"I remember trying so hard, and failing. They would never invite me to go anywhere with them, and I remember asking if I could come. I know this was obnoxious, and looking back on it, I feel extremely embarrassed. I once asked if I could go to the movies with them and one girl answered, 'Well, the movies are a public place, and we can't STOP you from going. And we can't STOP you from sitting with us...' and I knew that meant I wasn't wanted.

"When I would try to enter a conversation with them, they would start talking about something I knew nothing about, and when I would ask one of them to explain it to me, they would say, 'Oh... it's complicated.' This isn't really meanness; it's more exclusion, which can be viewed as meanness.

"This year I came up with a new approach for handling things like these. I realized that if people do not want to be my friend, it's okay. There isn't anything wrong with me. Self-satisfaction does not come from others around you...it comes from inside you.

"Once I realized this, I realized that I had nothing in common with these people. I had to face it—I was not made to be in the 'popular' clique, but I am still an adequate human being. I made friends with people who wanted to be my friends, and who didn't go out of their way to exclude me. Even though I am farther away from the popular clique than I have ever been, I am also happier than I have ever been, and that's what matters." Sasha, 13

Sasha's realization about her own happiness is pretty amazing. She saw all the cruelty and competition for what it really was: a waste of energy. She realized that the real secret to happiness doesn't come from being popular, and it certainly doesn't come from other people thinking highly of you (though that is nice sometimes). The real secret to being happy comes from feeling good about yourself, and liking yourself for who you are.

Being mean to other people will never really make you feel better about yourself. In fact, if you really think about this behavior, you'll see that it actually makes you feel worse. How can you be happy and satisfied about treating your friends—or anyone—badly? Not to mention the fact that your nastiness sets the tone around you, so you are only contributing to a culture that hurts you.

**What can we do about it?**

I know—yet again we have another huge problem that seems to have no solution. It seems that no matter what, girls will do mean things to each other. But there are definitely a number of ways we can deal with this problem.

Our first step is to do our very best to end our contribution to it. Every time we criticize someone else, especially when we do it harshly, we're adding to the climate of competition. Every time we purposely exclude someone from our plans, we're making the world a meaner place. The Golden Rule applies directly here—do to others as you would have them do to you. In other words, **treat other people the way you want to be treated yourself**.

***

Imagine how it would feel to be the other girl when you're mean to her. Or better yet, remember how it felt when it happened to you yesterday. The only way we can expect to be treated nicely by others is to lead by example, and to set the tone of niceness around us.

I know this may seem unrealistic. You're probably thinking that no matter what, no matter how nice you are, people will be mean to you. This may be true. There are some girls who, no matter what, will be pretty cruel to those around them. So, **don't be friends with mean girls**. They aren't worth your time.

***

Sometimes it's not possible to avoid nasty girls, because they are in your circle of friends, or because you go to a really small school and there are not too many other people to hang out with. If this is the case, **call them out**. Tell these girls that their behavior is ridiculous, and you want to be their friend but you don't know why they talk to you the way they do. Tell them that it is unbecoming of them to be so ruthless, and that not only does it make you feel bad, but it makes them look bad. I know it seems hard to say these things, and it is, but I think that with enough practice, you can do it. Try to stay calm and rational when you confront people about their mean behavior.

***

Sometimes, calling mean girls out is too intimidating, or simply doesn't work. If meanness continues to happen, try to **let it roll off your back**. I know it's hard, but you can do it! Mean behavior makes us second-guess ourselves, lowers our self-esteem, and prevents us from being the strong, confident women we deserve to be. That's exactly what it's meant to do. Often, the reason girls are obnoxious to you is because they are jealous of you—of your confidence, your beauty, or your inner strength. Remember that the next time you are upset about something a 'friend' has done to you.

## Confronting bullies

Most bullies think that it's okay to behave the way they do because no one calls them out. I remember feeling really frustrated about this because it was obvious to everyone that bullying was happening, yet no one would say anything. I often wanted to confront mean girls. It was really hard, though, because when people get called out, they are likely to defend themselves, and pretend their behavior is no big deal.

If you decide to confront a mean girl, try to do it right after she has done something cruel, so you have evidence of her behavior that she can't deny. This might be challenging, because in the heat of the moment, you are probably upset and angry. The last thing you want to do is lose your cool in a conversation like this. So try to think about what you might say to a bully, then when the opportunity arises to confront her, you are ready. Sometimes it's more effective to take the bullying patiently, and then stick it to the bully by calmly pointing out how ridiculous her behavior is. Check this out:

"I was watching one of my best friends pick on someone who she thought was less 'cool' than her. My friend would say the meanest things to this girl, and make up rumors about her, just to see if she could make her cry. The girl being picked on never did cry or even flinch when she got put down. Then, one day when this girl was getting picked on, she finally got the courage to answer back and said, 'Just because you are insecure about being popular doesn't mean you have to be like this. Just because you are jealous of me doesn't mean you have to make fun of me. Get over yourself.'

"My friend just stood there, and then everyone started to laugh at her. I felt bad, but by this point I didn't care enough to comfort her. She had said too much and had gone too far. In the end, my friend stopped making fun of people, and realized she had lost a lot of friends because of her behavior. The girl that was picked on is now one of my closest friends." Amy, 15

If you remind yourself of your inner strength, you can handle yourself gracefully, and simply ignore the mean behavior. Do you really want to be friends with people who aren't going to treat you as you deserve to be treated?

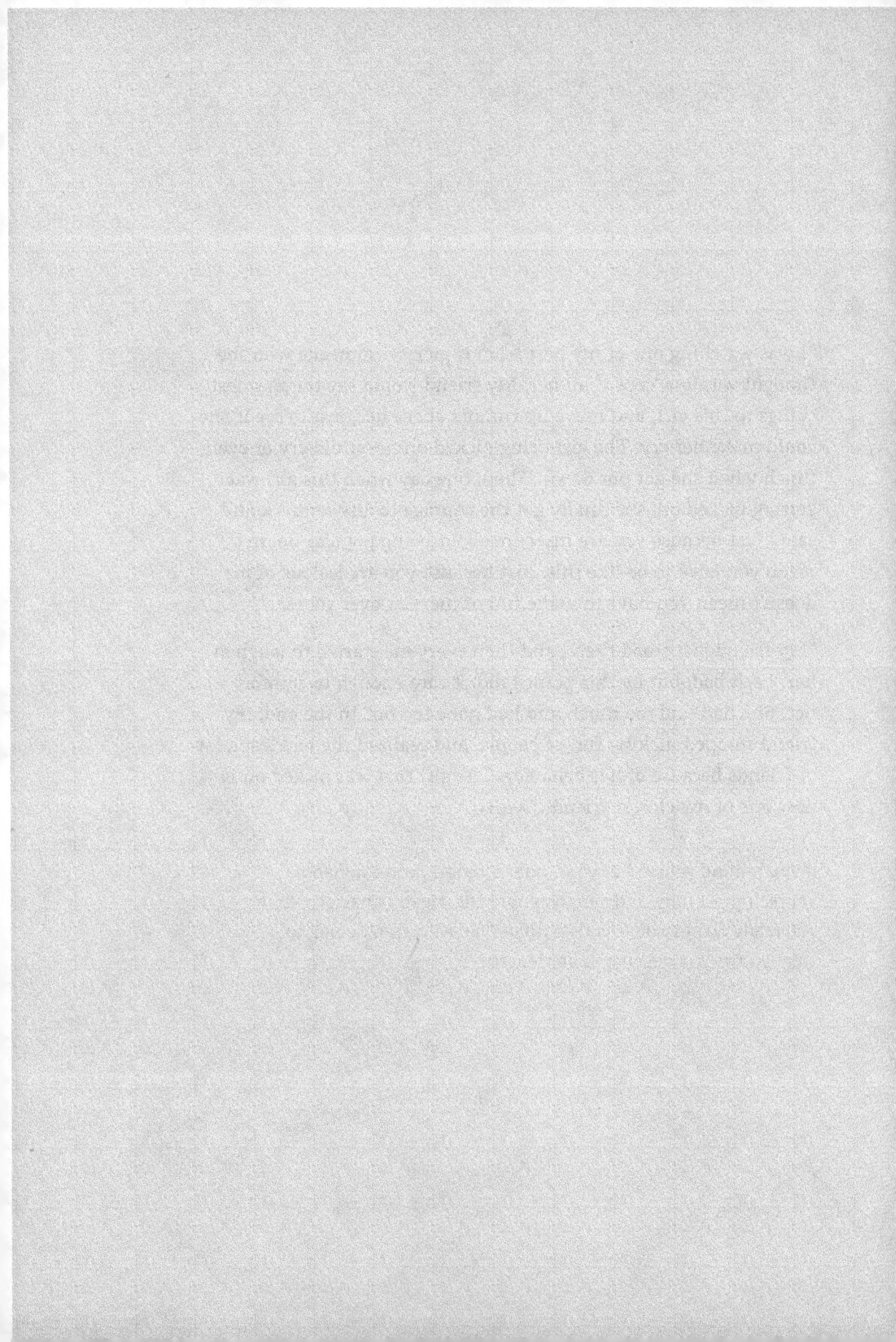

# FIVE

# How Do I Want to be Treated?
# How Do I Want to Treat Others?

The way we treat each other is directly connected to the way we treat ourselves. Remember the Golden Rule—that we should do to others as we'd like them to do to us. But it's easy to forget that there are two sides to that idea. On one hand, we need to treat other people the way we ourselves expect to be treated. We should be nice because we want other people to be nice to us. On the other hand, we need to take responsibility for our own well-being in our relationships and spend time with people who treat us the way we think we deserve to be treated. It's easy to forget that second part—that we should think

## Meanness quiz

> Do your friends say things that they know will make you upset?

> Do your friends sometimes leave you out of their plans?

> Do your friends criticize you for the way you dress, look, or act?

If you answered yes to any of these questions, you are a normal teenage girl. As we discussed in the last chapter, many girls deal with meanness from their friends on a fairly regular basis. While this isn't treatment we should have to accept, it's important to be aware of the fact it happens all the time, and to many people. It's even more important to remember that despite this obnoxious treatment, you are still a beautiful person, inside and out, and deserve to be surrounded by people who will respect you, and love you for who you are, not for who they think you should be.

about how our friends act toward us, and decide whether their behavior is acceptable. It's especially easy to forget this when we are in a phase of our lives when we might not be so nice to ourselves. It is up to us to decide what we are willing to put up with, and from whom.

I've already told you about my friends who made fun of me, and made me feel bad about myself. I shouldn't have stayed as close friends with them as I did. I could have thought more about myself and my needs in those relationships. Instead, I chose to try as hard as I could to remain popular, risking my own happiness. Looking back, I think that I would have been a lot happier as a less popular person whose friends were actually nice to her. I had unhealthy friendships because I didn't have the confidence to stand up to my friends, and tell them how I felt about the way they treated me. I also didn't believe that I could make new friends. I was too scared to change things, and honestly didn't really think it was possible. I didn't recognize that I deserved better.

I don't think that this experience is unique to me. There are lots of girls out there who are in different kinds of relationships in which they get treated badly. Some of those relationships are friendships, some are dating relationships, and some are simply acquaintances, both boys and girls, who make fun of us, and just generally make us feel bad about ourselves. Why do we take it? I'm not really sure. But I think we are afraid to leave the group, or maybe we think we don't deserve better. We live in a society that tells girls that the woman's role is to be a pleaser, rather than to do what she wants. All over the media, we see women acting in all sorts of ridiculous ways in order to attract guys, or to get the approval of their peers. What we see a lot less often are strong, confident women and girls acting in ways that show them being true to themselves.

"There are lots of ways that girls are mean to each other. Girls usually exclude other girls from their group. If they think that someone is not cool, then they don't want to be with them in front of their friends. They ignore them, but if they need them, then they are nice to them, especially if they need help with homework, or something like that.

"Girls also spread rumors about each other. Sometimes girls spread rumors to get back at someone for something they did. They want this girl to be humiliated; that way they'll be even with this person. Sometimes girls spread rumors because they want to have something to talk about. Girls want to be like, 'Oh, you like that rumor? I made it up.' Girls want to point out something humiliating or bad about a girl to point out that they themselves are not like that. They just want to do whatever it takes to be 'cool.'" **Rebecca, 13**

## Where do we learn to be the way we are?

I strongly believe that this message—that it is more important to get the approval of those around us than it is to be who we really are—has a profound impact on our society, and especially on adolescent girls. We put ourselves in relationships that hide our real selves—or don't let us discover who our real selves are at all.

"One time I was trying to fit in, and Jasmine and Ashley were teasing this girl [named Azah]. They were teasing her because Jasmine was going to fight [Azah], and she was scared.... Azah was so intimidated that she stayed in the principal's office all day, and when she came out, she was trying to act all bad. We were mad that she hid from the situation, and talked about it at lunch. Then someone decided to start throwing staples at her. I only threw two staples, but I apologize for it every day.

"It makes me sad to think about the way I used to be. I also feel bad for all the hurt I caused in some people's lives, especially my girl Azah's. We are so tight now, we talk every day. That girl is like my best friend." **Chanece, 13**

Looking back on her experience, Chanece can see that the things she did to her friend did not make her proud, nor did they help build a positive relationship. She was pressured into throwing staples—a dangerous activity—at a girl she now considers her best friend! I think that if Chanece had felt stronger about herself as a person, and didn't feel that she needed the approval of her friends so badly, she probably wouldn't have been so mean to Azah.

But it's one thing for me to say that, and an entirely different thing for Chanece to actually be in the mental place to think about herself that way. All people, not just adolescents, are influenced by the opinions of those around them. We want people to like us, to think we are smart, pretty, interesting, fun, whatever. In different stages of life, we are willing to sell ourselves out to different degrees in order to get this kind of approval from our peers.

"When I was considered a 'mean girl,' it was because I tagged along with my friend Chloe. We did mean things like kicking people out of changing rooms, or pulling people's pants down (things I did when I was a lot younger). After a while I realized that I was only doing that so I would be accepted. When you're at such a young age you don't really know who you are, and I guess you could say that almost everyone goes through a stage where they're mean to other people. People who are still mean are probably doing it because they're insecure about themselves. Don't be a follower!!!!" Jennie, 14

As an adult, I am much more confident than I was as an adolescent. I am not interested in hanging out with people who try to make me do things that I don't want to do. I am also not willing to forget who I am, and how much I love myself, in order to win someone else's approval.

In middle school and high school, I wasn't so sure of myself. I felt insecure all the time. I wanted people to like me, and developed a mask that helped me become popular, even though I didn't like the mask myself, now that I think about it. I did what I thought would make other people like me, which sometimes meant being nasty to others, or looking down on myself. I was pretty out of touch with the person I really was, and the kinds of friendships I really wanted. I wish I'd had a clearer sense of what was actually going on.

## Ask yourself

> Am I proud of the way I behave?

> Do I treat other people in ways that I would want to be treated?

> Have I hurt anyone today? This week?

> Do I feel like I owe anyone an apology for my behavior?

> Who is the person I want to be?

> Name three qualities of a good friend. Do I possess these qualities?

> Do I model them for others?

> How can I be a better friend?

## Peer pressure: how does it affect us?

"Peer pressure is like a mild version of blackmail. Everyone has peer pressure in their lives. I have these friends, and they always pressure me into saying things I don't want to say, and when I try to say no, they say it's just a joke. Meanwhile I am thinking, well, if it's just a joke, then why do I have to say it and not you? It always aggravates me when people are telling me to do things I don't want to do, and they just make fun of me if I don't do it. But when I do, they will make fun of me for making a fool of myself, and when I say you made me do it, then they'll say, YOU DIDN'T HAVE TO DO IT! So, in a way, peer pressure creates somewhat of a lose-lose situation.

"In my opinion, there are three levels of peer pressure. The first level happens among friends, when they make each other say or do something funny that will sound or look idiotic. The second level of peer pressure is when someone has to say something hurtful to look cool and be friends with certain people. The third level is hurting someone physically to get what you want. When you are the one who is pressuring someone into something, you don't really realize it, because you think you are poking fun at people, but you could be seriously ruining someone's self-esteem." Shabnam, 13

Peer pressure is a vicious element of adolescent relationships. Friends make each other do things that they probably wouldn't do otherwise, and in the process, they hurt themselves and each other. This kind of pressure manifests in many ways, and results in us maintaining relationships that aren't good for us. This is not to say that any time there is peer pressure the relationship is unhealthy. But there is a limit to what I think we should consider acceptable. Our limits depend entirely on how we see ourselves. If we are less confident, then we are willing to let people push us around more.

I can't overemphasize how important it is for us to try as hard as we can to think clearly about who we are, and what is important to us. Peer pressure can make people do things that are not only nasty and hurtful, but dangerous.

"Peer pressure is that girl puking up her lunch in the bathroom stall. Peer pressure is the normally A+ student smoking behind the science class he is supposed to be in. Peer pressure is the 14-year-old girl being raped at her big sister's high school party. Peer pressure is the guy stuffing money into a stripper's bra even though he feels no attraction to her. Peer pressure is the 17-year-old girl feeling ashamed of her first female kiss, and of liking it. Peer pressure is the boy being put into the ground as a result of driving home drunk." Medina, 13

The results of peer pressure are scary, and Medina really breaks it down. There are times when we are pressured to look a certain way, so we put ourselves at risk, not eating, or puking up our food, or taking laxatives, or over-exercising. Pressure tells us that it's not cool to do well in school, so we skip class and risk our health by smoking cigarettes. We think that we have to be sexual in order to be cool, and we go to parties where the kids are older and more experienced than we are, and we get hurt. We think of women as objects, because that's what our culture tells us to do. Men tend to approve of women objectifying themselves, because they think they are supposed to. The guys are afraid that if they don't, they're not normal.

Peer pressure is all about defining what is normal, and making people feel stupid for being anything else. The girl who kisses another girl—and likes it—thinks she isn't normal because she hears her friends make fun of lesbians and gay people. The boy in the car accident may never have had a drink if his friends hadn't pressured him to. And if they were really his friends, they never would have let him get behind the wheel of his car. Imagine how they feel now.

**What can we do about it?**

There are clearly lots of different ways in which peer pressure affects us, and each demands a different type of response.

We've already talked about cruelty and the pressure to be mean, about how important it is to know ourselves, and to speak the truth, especially when we feel pressured. I know this might feel like it is next to impossible, especially when it seems that if you don't go along with what the cool kids are doing, you will be an outcast forever. The way I think we can handle this, though, is to **really believe we are okay and cool the way we are**.

"Peer pressure is one of the core reasons why we make decisions. Whether you're an adult, a young child or a teenager, peer pressure affects you every day. I blame peer pressure for so much that goes on in our world, both good and bad. However, there is no doubt in my mind that it should not be the factor we rely on to get things done. So many people around me lose their individuality to fit into a group, or depend on pressure put on by others to make decisions for them about what they do and who they are, instead of coming to terms with their true beliefs and values.

"I must admit that peer pressure has played a huge role in my life. As much as I try to stay consistent with my beliefs, there are many times when I abandon my perspective to fit in with a group. I've gotten in a lot of trouble for just that, and I believe that is one of the main reasons I'm beginning to choose to stand for what I believe, instead of always going with the group.

"Everyone likes to fit into groups, to belong to a community. To me, peer pressure is not always bad. I think oftentimes it is the reason wonderful things happen in our lives. Certain aspects of life that I have grown to love were not there in the beginning, and I only discovered them because I was pressured into doing so.

"Some things people try to drag you into are bad and dangerous. In the world of teenagers, there is often a lot of pressure around drugs and alcohol. With pressures like these, you must learn to resist. With peer pressure, I think you must decide which pressures are good, and which are bad. You must be adventurous, but when it all comes down to it, stick with what you know to be right, and what you truly believe." Amelia, 13

I couldn't have said it better myself. There are definitely some kinds of pressure that open our minds to new and exciting things. But it's important to be able to **distinguish positive pressure from negative pressure**, which makes us lose sight of our true selves.

We've talked about friends and how important it is to remember how we deserve to be treated in our friendships. In the next chapters we'll think about this concept even more, about how peer pressure affects the different areas of our lives and the ways we think about ourselves.

Overall though, we have to remember: **each of us is unique and special. We deserve to feel that way all the time**. Peer pressure plays on our insecurities, takes advantage of us when we forget how unique and special we are. We do the things we are pressured into doing because we want to feel loved. But really—do we want to be loved by people who will only love us if we act the way they want us to? I want my friends to love and respect me for who I am, not for who they think I should be.

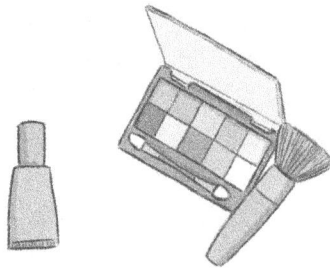

# SIX

# #Gorgeous

I started working with girls over 20 years ago, before social media existed. I have witnessed the ways in which social dynamics have completely changed for teenagers with the invention of Facebook, Instagram, Snapchat, all the rest, and, of course, social media's best partner in crime, the smartphone. The impact has been devastating. I am not exaggerating.

I have seen the ways in which girls' lives have been turned upside down because of social media. I am not only talking about specific cases of girls who were cyberbullied, or whose pictures were shared widely without their permission, though of course this has happened, and when it does, it's awful. Those kinds of specific incidents are omnipresent and very serious. But I want to talk about the overall impact the invention of social media has had on dynamics among teens in general, and on the lives of girls in particular.

I repeat, the impact has been devastating. I am not exaggerating.

And your parents, who will NEVER understand the ways in which you use these media, aren't really in the best position to give you guidance. Parents have good intentions and they want to help, but they are struggling to find the tools with which to support you in your relationship with these confusing inventions. These technologies—the smartphone, the Internet and all it brings with it—came into our lives with a bang and we humans are scrambling to figure out how to navigate the complexities of learning to safely conduct ourselves in this new world. I can't tell you how many parents have asked me what to do and how to respond to their kids' use of social media. The list of questions feels endless:

"Should we place limits on screen time? How?"

"Should we check our kids' profiles? When?"

"What should we say if we see something that concerns us?"

I respect your parents' intentions, and their efforts to help you. However, in general I don't think it's good for any parent-child relationship for the parent to be checking their kids' profiles — or to be doing anything that breaks trust between children and their parents. I would like to think that you are mature enough to know what you want to post and why, and that you are able to make good decisions about social media as well as many other aspects of your life. Chances are, your parents are not going to be there when you are offered a drink or when you need to make a decision about sex. This means that you need to be able to make good decisions on your own, and that your parents need to trust you to do so. The same is true of our relationship with social media. That being said, let's recognize that we do need the support and guidance of our parents — in many complicated situations — but we also need to learn how to guide and monitor ourselves.

I believe that you can take the situation into your own hands. I know you don't need your mom or dad looking over your shoulder each time you post! You can observe and understand how your time online makes you feel and from that understanding, YOU can decide what you want your relationship with social media to look like.

Technological inventions have literally changed the world, changed the way humans live on this earth—in ways that are revolutionary and open worlds of possibility, and also in ways that could lead to our demise. You are a pioneer generation. You are truly breaking evolutionary ground for humanity as you try to define what a healthy relationship with technology looks like. Because you are the first generation to be born into this technological revolution, to be born into the world of social media, you are also taking the first step in defining what healthy relationships with technology can look like for youth. When we look at extreme examples—someone who obsessively checks her profiles and spends hours doing her hair and makeup for a selfie, someone who asks for nude pics and shares them widely without permission—we can clearly see what UNHEALTHY relationships with social media look like. What we are faced with is the challenge of deciding and defining what HEALTHY relationships look like. So how do we make good choices on our own? First, we need to understand how we use social media, and how it affects us.

### How does social media actually impact us?

Now, don't get me wrong—I use social media too, and I think it has many advantages. I think it's amazing how we can stay connected with people so far away, and it's incredible how political movements can gain ground through online messaging. But I also think that it's upsetting that social media has led us to be so obsessed with our image. And that's not the only way social media negatively affects us: I also see that what the experts say is true—the more I go on social media, the more unhappy I feel. Why?

Keep in mind, my purpose in asking questions is not to make us feel upset or angry about how hard it is to live with the effects of social media. On the contrary—I want to emphasize the opposite: I am bringing up the severity of the impact of social media so that we can understand how checking our Instagram or Facebook or Snapchat or whatever pages all the time makes us feel. If we can see that, then we can take control and be smart about how we use these platforms, instead of letting them control us. That's the key.

## Like!

More than anything, social media has impacted girls' self-confidence. The way we see ourselves, or better said, the way we look at ourselves through the lens we use to decide how we want to be seen, has changed completely. All of a sudden, image has become THE MOST IMPORTANT aspect of who we are.

Certainly, our external appearance was important before social media. No doubt. But something about the way in which we are posting pictures and waiting for people to LIKE them has made us even more image-obsessed, particularly with images in which women and girls are very, very sexualized.

In her book *American Girls: Social Media and the Secret Lives of Teenagers*, Nancy Jo Sales writes that, "On social media, things which once might have been considered outrageous or disturbing come to seem normal very quickly through widespread repetition."[1] In other words, something that might have once seemed extreme has become normal because it's all over the place. True enough—do you think that it was always acceptable to ask for nude pictures? To post photos of ourselves looking extremely provocative, as though we are asking for sex?

"Sometimes, my mood gets better or worse based on the number of likes I get on a picture, or the comments I receive."
**Amit, 18**

It's become completely normal for us to post photos and wait for people to respond—to tell us that we are pretty enough, sexy enough, enough of whatever it is that will make others like us. And our moods are deeply affected by others' reactions.

Sales explores the origin of social media and traces the like back to "hot or not," a concept "first seen online in 2000 with the launch of the photo-rating site Hot or Not...[started by two software engineers] after an argument about whether a certain woman was attractive, or 'hot.'" This idea also led to FaceMash, another site for rating photos, created by Mark Zuckerberg before he invented Facebook in 2004. "The two founders of YouTube...[also men] have said that Hot or Not was the inspiration for what they originally thought would just be a video version of the game, as well. Much of the culture of social media is, in a way, an ongoing expression of 'hot or not,' liking or rejecting people and things, and the physical appeal of women and girls."[2]

So basically, when someone likes your picture, they are saying that they think you are hot. While this is not true all of the time, all it takes is a quick look at comments on photos posted online and you'll see words like 'sexy,' 'gorgeous,' and 'looking good.' This reflects the fact that, often, the main thing people are responding to in photos is how hot, or not, the subject looks. And, think about it, we use these media all the time. Many girls have said to me that they are online 24/7—I am not sure if they literally are, but if they are saying that, I understand that regardless of the number of hours they actually spend online, it feels to them like it's 24/7. This means that 24 hours a day, 7 days a week, they are entrenched in this world that is very much about how hot we are. OUCH. That is definitely not easy.

## Give me a break...please!

A 16-year-old girl in Los Angeles told journalist Nancy Jo Sales that "social media is destroying our lives." So why wouldn't they just go off it? "Because then we would have no life," her friend said.[3] I don't think anyone can argue with the fact that social media has changed our culture, has changed the way we socialize. This is particularly true for teenagers, who were born into a world where this phenomenon already existed.

It is really important for you to understand that the adults in your life do not understand the way you use social media and, chances are, they never will. For the generation older than you, my generation, social media came into being once we had already developed most of the skills of socializing—in person—with others. For you, virtual socializing has always been a part of your world. Adults who use social media are generally using it to stay connected with friends and family or share news, but it is an addition to the social lives they

> "The fact that I have social media means that I give other people the possibility of reacting to my pictures and posts, which basically means that there is no one who is protecting me 100%, ever." Eva, 14

already had beforehand. Of course, that does not mean that just because people are older they make responsible use of these networks: adults are also struggling with this new wave of technology. For example, there is a whole new issue that has emerged around posting pictures of your kids, or promoting your own kids through social media, a phenomenon largely called 'sharenting'—parents who are just sharing too much. We are facing a literal cultural epidemic: our society is actually ill from using social media and we all need to get this whole situation under control. But, our focus is teenagers, so we'll leave sharenting and other such issues to another discussion.

For your generation, social media has been an integral part of socializing for your entire lives. As I said earlier, this means that it's up to you to define what that means and how to use these media in a healthy way. Remember, you are PIONEERS—defining humanity's first steps in a new relationship with technology.

Leaving aside for a minute the physical impact of constantly checking our phones, day and night, the idea of being glued to these machines 24 hours a day is REALLY INTENSE. We can easily see the intensity when we are talking about a person whose work infiltrates every moment of their day, like the mom who is answering emails at the dinner table, or the dad who sends texts while he's watching his daughter's basketball game. I think we can all agree that we need to take breaks from our work life. The same is true for our social lives. If I am constantly in communication with my friends, or with anyone for that matter, when do I have time for myself? And more simply, maybe, than time for myself, when do I have a break from this crazy social world that is unfolding around me all the time? When do I have time to actually relax and integrate all that I am experiencing? We can't live without any down time!

I remember a wide variety of uncomfortable social situations I experienced as a teenager (many of which I have shared in this book). I am not going to repeat them here, but I will say that no matter what happened at school, at some point each day I went home. I can't say that I was able to completely leave the social situation behind when I left school, but I did have some kind of break. In the safety of my room I was far away from all the drama that unfolded in the halls of my middle school and high school life.

Since the invention of the smartphone, that break no longer exists. Social dynamics continue to unfold well into the night, and stress about what will happen the next day continues to build. I used to get really stressed out about going to school the day after I had an argument with a friend on the phone; I can only imagine how upsetting it is to go to school after something has unfolded online.

"My phone is constantly with me, not just because of Instagram or Snapchat but also because I'm getting messages and calls—people need to be able to get in touch with me."

Ma'ayan, 13

## Sophia's story

I first made an Instagram and Snapchat account at the impressionable age of 11. I started off using Instagram to post funny pictures of me and my friends. I wasn't worrying about the amount of likes or comments I received. That quickly changed the next year, in 7th grade, when EVERYONE had an Instagram and Snapchat account. Before I knew it, social media had taken over my entire life. I was desperate to have the same type of Instagram account as other girls, who seemed beautiful, popular, and fun. I spent hours upon hours looking at other girls' Instagram accounts and trying to achieve the same perfection.

Soon enough, the sweet little girl who carried around a book wherever she went became a superficial, insecure girl who carried around her iPhone wherever she went. I was obsessed and addicted in every way possible. Addicted to the likes, to the comments, to the Snapchats, but most of all, to my Instagram page, which I had learned to edit perfectly. Whenever I was feeling down, I would post a picture. As the likes streamed in, my confidence was instantly boosted and I was happy again. If I posted a picture that didn't get enough likes (by my standards), I was in a horrible mood and rude to everyone around me. I constantly relied on the validation of others through their likes and comments.

The question I still ask myself today is why and how did I let a smartphone app control my entire life, confidence, and happiness levels? Maybe I'll never know. My older sister and parents warned me that I was addicted and tried to help, but it was a lost cause. I had to come to my own conclusions about just how unhealthy my relationship with social media was in order for any real change to occur.

It all happened little by little. In 8th grade, I became more active and participated in more outdoor activities which significantly decreased the amount of time I spent on social media. I was instantly happier. By 9th grade, I found more and more things that I really enjoyed, like running, singing, and volunteering, all of which I did regularly. I felt fit and happy. I was growing into my own person.

By 10th grade, I had a set group of friends, activities and was doing really well in school. I felt like I had it all. But HAVING it all wasn't enough; for whatever reason I felt the need to SHOW the world I had it all.

By actively seeking to post Snapchat stories and Instagram posts of my happy life, in the long run, I lost happiness. I stopped running as much and put less effort into school because I wasted more time online. I suddenly felt that my happy life wasn't as good as others' lives, and constantly felt like I had to improve my life based upon what others had, did, and looked like. And again, I faced the issue of feeling that I wasn't getting enough likes. The more I displayed my happiness online, the more unhappy I truly felt.

Then, in the summer after 10th grade, I went to Nepal, on a program where phones are banned. I had no phone for four weeks and lived in a rural village where there was no running water or any degree of modern technology. The people were the happiest people I had ever met, and it was truly the happiest I had ever been in my entire life. When I returned home to my iPhone, I barely wanted to even see it.

I was disgusted with who I was with my phone, but knew, eventually, I would have to start using it again. I logged onto Instagram but was quickly overwhelmed and threw my phone to the ground.

Slowly, I got into a routine where I used Instagram for my own pleasure, not to please others. I don't post photos to impress other people, I post photos I enjoy. Instagram and Snapchat are just another aspect of my life, and I don't care what others think, how many likes or comments I receive. Yes, I could just delete my account, but I'd rather use it for good than give it up all together. After all, there are some positive aspects of having Instagram. Now, I go on Instagram to look at accounts that help me grow, have a laugh, or keep in touch with long distance friends. I stay away from accounts of people that I know I will inevitably compare myself to and end up feeling bad, and I only allow myself to go on Instagram during the weekends.

I am currently the happiest I've ever been since I've gotten an Instagram (besides in Nepal), and there is no doubt in my mind that my happiness directly correlates to my healthy relationship with social media. It's unfortunate I had to go through those painful years of obsessing over Instagram, but at least now I can help others learn from my mistakes.

**Sophia, 16**

## More screen time, less happiness

Almost across the board, experts say that spending more time on screen, particularly on social media, directly results in lower levels of happiness.

"The twin rise of the smartphone and social media has caused an earthquake of a magnitude we've not seen in a very long time, if ever. There is compelling evidence that the devices we've placed in young people's hands are having profound effects on their lives—and making them seriously unhappy. Teens who spend more time than average on screen activities are more likely to be unhappy, and those who spend more time than average on nonscreen activities are more likely to be happy.

"There's not a single exception. All screen activities are linked to less happiness, and all nonscreen activities are linked to more happiness. Eighth-graders who spend ten or more hours a week on social media are 56 percent more likely to say they're unhappy than those who devote less time to social media. Admittedly, ten hours a week is a lot. But those who spend six to nine hours a week on social media are still 47 percent more likely to say they are unhappy than those who use social media even less...

"Teens who visit social-networking sites every day but see their friends in person less frequently are the most likely to agree with the statements 'A lot of times I feel lonely,' 'I often feel left out of things' and 'I often wish I had more good friends.' Teens' feelings of loneliness spiked in 2013 and have remained high since."[4]

Whoa. And that's just one article. Before writing this chapter, I read quite a bit of research, all of which says more or less the same thing: spending more time on social media is causing more unhappiness. And teens are nearly obsessively checking their profiles, spending an average of nine hours online daily, and around 30 percent of that (three hours) on social media sites. Every day.[5] 92 percent of teens go online daily—including 24 percent who say they go online "almost constantly."[6] That can add up to a lot of unhappiness.

## Some statistics about teens and technology[7]

> In 2015, the Pew Research Center did an extensive study about teens and technology. They found that 92% of teens go online daily—including 24% who say they go online "almost constantly."

> Three-quarters (76%) of teens use social media, and 81% of older teens use the sites, compared with 68% of teens 13 to 14.

> Girls are far more likely than boys to use visually-oriented platforms, while boys are more likely to use video games. Of the teens in the study, 61% of the girls use Instagram as compared to 44% of boys. 51% of girls use Snapchat, compared to 31% of boys.

Again, it is important for me to say that I use social media too, and as I said before, there are aspects of the Internet that I really appreciate. For example, there's a good chance that some of you are reading this book because you or someone you know heard about it through social media.

I live far away from many people I love very much, and I can see what's happening in their lives. And I can share with them too. That said, I do think that it's risky, especially for teens, to put our whole lives online for all the world to see. It's important to be selective and share smartly, both publicly and via emails or messages. With that, I also LIKE seeing what people are up to and can easily get sucked in to check out others' lives. And when I do, I see that what the experts say is true—the more I go on social media, the more unhappy I feel.

Why?

These technologies allow us to share messages widely—and that is very powerful. But what are the messages we are spreading? And how do we integrate those messages into our lives?

## Comparing myself to others

How many times have you gotten bummed out from seeing other people's profiles—how happy they are with their friends, how good they look—but honestly, do you think that those images represent the REAL person?

"When you go online, you are comparing your inside with someone else's outside."[8] It's true. The life that we show on our profiles is, by no means, a full picture of the life we are living. Yes, there are people who update literally all the time, and we know about the meals they ate and exactly where they have been over the past 48 hours. And there are also plenty of posts about challenges that people are facing. But overwhelmingly, we are posting images of ourselves that we LIKE. We are posting stories and pictures that show the positive sides of our lives. We are showing the self that we want to be (or that we think others want us to be), and not necessarily the self that we really are.

I am not even talking about filters and the ways in which we can literally change the way we look in our photos. I am simply talking about what we choose to post. When I go online, I see pictures of my friends looking beautiful, enjoying their lives, doing fun things, being proud of their kids, loving their partners...

## Being safe online

The Internet is an amazing invention. No doubt. It also presents us with certain potential risks, and being safe in the face of those risks means being aware. Some very important things to keep in mind:

> Be extra aware when you are communicating online with people you don't know well. Don't give out your real name, or any information that could help someone find you. This includes your school, your address, etc. You wouldn't tell a random person on the street where you live: keep the same caution online.

> Just don't give your username or password to anyone. Period. If you do, others can post and pretend they are you, and this can lead to lots of trouble.

> Remember that what you post online becomes available for everyone to see. Think about that when you share pics, or when you consider leaving someone a rude comment. This is especially important to remember if you are considering posting risqué pics: too many stories that began with risqué pics have ended badly, such as pics being shared widely after a breakup, or who knows what else. Don't post anything that you would not want going viral.

"If someone asks you to send them sexual pictures, be very suspicious—and don't do it."[9] If you are asked by someone you know, you can tell them why you are not willing. If you are asked by someone you don't know, tell your parents so that they are aware of the situation and can look after your safety.

> Don't meet up in person with people you met online. It's just not safe, especially because online people can pretend to be someone they are not. If you really think you have made a new friend and you really do want to meet them, talk to your parents so that they can help you organize a safe way to meet. Either go with one of them, or with a friend, and meet in a public place. That way, you can always walk away if the situation gets creepy.

And yes, that is a part of our lives, but we are also sometimes sad, angry, hurt, or disappointed; we struggle to find love, we don't always look our best, we just simply aren't always those picture-perfect lives we try to share.

Yet, when we go online and browse through social media, we forget. We see images of lives we wish we had, and—even if we personally know the people behind the images, and we know the truth about their experiences—we fail to remember that those people have lives very much like ours: they too are sometimes sad, angry, hurt or disappointed, and they are far less likely to share those moments online.

A survey of over 1000 young people in the UK "found that 35 percent of girls aged 11-21 said their biggest worry online was comparing themselves and their lives with others."[10]

"Sometimes when I see someone pretty on Instagram, or someone who is wearing nice clothes, I am jealous. I also want to look like her and have the same clothes." Ma'ayan, 13

## Some thoughts about Snapchat

Snapchat can be a helpful tool to stay in touch and send funny pictures to your friends, but there are some very negative aspects to the app. First off, teens can post Snapchat stories (which all of their Snapchat contacts can view for 24 hours) that depict picture-perfect lives and make others feel constantly left out. No one ever posts something less than pleasant on their story, and most teens (mostly girls) spend an absurd amount of time making their story 'just right' so that the post looks perfect, but not like they actually tried too hard to make it look that way. They obsess over who views their story as it is a sign that people care about you.

Snapchat is also a vessel for many fake and toxic friendships to form through the feature of having a 'streak.' A streak is when you snapchat someone every single day, and the number of consecutive days you've snapchatted them appears next to their contact name. The higher the number is, the more impressive the streak is and the closer the friendship seems. Streaks are a sign of popularity and power. The more streaks a teen has, the more cool and well-liked they seem to others. It becomes a competition as to who has the most streaks, which pushes teens to snapchat more and more people so they have as many streaks as possible, even if they don't actually know or like the person. The basis of many toxic friendships begins with the words "let's start a streak!" in which two individuals make this commitment to send many snaps to one another daily. They appear to have a lively friendship, yet they hardly communicate at all in person. This is a really problematic aspect of how my generation forms relationships and develops social skills.

Another threatening aspect of Snapchat is your 'Snapchat score.' Your Snapchat score is a composite number of how many snapchats you've sent, and how many snapchats you've received, which is available for all of your Snapchat contacts to see. The higher your score is the more popular and cool you seem. It is socially unacceptable to have a low score on Snapchat, and if you do you're seen as inferior to those with a higher score regardless of the individuals' true personalities. The Snapchat score component causes teens to snapchat one another relentlessly so that their score is as high as possible.

Your Snapchat score and the amount of streaks you have is like a grade for your social life (only even more anxiety inducing than your actual grades at times because everyone is able to see your score). Everyone compares their streaks and their Snapchat score to others', which causes them to feel like a loser at least once in a while, if not all the time.

Overall, Snapchat is just another app that tests your popularity and confidence which can ultimately make you feel extremely lonely or unpopular, not only because of how many streaks you have and your Snapchat score, but also from seeing others' stories of their seemingly perfect lives.

**Sophia, 16**

Researchers have proposed a new phenomenon called "Facebook depression," defined as depression that develops when preteens and teens spend a great deal of time on social media sites, such as Facebook, and then begin to exhibit classic symptoms of depression.[11]

A study published in 2014 reflects on the connection between Facebook use and eating disorders:

"Social media sites, such as Facebook, merge two factors that influence risk for eating disorders: media and peers. More frequent Facebook use was associated with greater disordered eating in a cross-sectional survey."[12] In other words, spending more time on Facebook increased the likelihood of developing an eating disorder. Why? Probably because of the dangerous way in which using Facebook (and other social media sites) combines the influence of media—which tells us to be sexy—and our peers—who are often judging us/being judged by us.

So we compare ourselves to friends and strangers/celebrities, get jealous, and feel inferior when we see positive, 'picture-perfect' lives on social media—forgetting that these photos are not accurate depictions of people's lives. That can be very dangerous for teens, who often feel pressured to look or act a certain way to fit in to a group or meet accepted standards.

## Online courage?

I think that we can all agree that many people will say things online that they would never say in real life. Sitting behind a phone or computer makes the interaction far less personal—even when we know the person we are chatting with—and makes us feel more detached from both what we say and the person to whom we are saying it.

This is pretty dangerous—the Internet allows us to be meaner/more sexual/more flirtatious than we probably would in real life; it allows us to be something we are not.

Some people take this so far as to literally pretend to be someone else online, which means we have to be very aware and careful when we are communicating virtually: even if we think we know who we are talking to, we may find ourselves speaking to someone who isn't who s/he says s/he is or who doesn't have our best interests at heart.

## I am left out...again

Social media has had an impact on all teens, but research has shown that girls are affected much more than boys. For girls in particular, social media is, in a way, the perfect platform for the unfolding of social dramas, especially mean behavior. What better way for someone to feel excluded—a classic dynamic that plays out among adolescent girls—than to see pictures of all her 'friends' having the 'best time' doing something she wasn't invited to join? "For all their power to link kids day and night, social media also exacerbate the age-old teen concern about being left out. Today's teens may go to fewer parties and spend less time together in person, but when they do congregate, they document their hangouts relentlessly—on Snapchat, Instagram, Facebook. Those not invited to come along are keenly aware of it."[13]

Remember Sasha's story from Chapter Four? "I saw in the TV shows and movies that the beautiful, popular girls were always happy, and everyone liked them or wanted to be them. I felt that the key to happiness was to be part of the 'popular' clique in our school. I started trying to be friends with this clique, but it backfired. Some days I would think to myself, 'Hey, I think they're starting to like me,' and the next day, when they completely excluded me, purposely, from their plans, I would think that I was inadequate, that something was wrong with me.

"I remember trying so hard, and failing. They would never invite me to go anywhere with them, and I remember asking if I could come. I know this was obnoxious, and looking back on it, I feel extremely embarrassed. I once asked if I could go to the movies with them and one girl answered, 'Well, the movies are a public place, and we can't STOP you from going. And we can't STOP you from sitting with us...' and I knew that meant I wasn't wanted, and I would go back to feeling inadequate."

Sasha was in the first girls' group I ever facilitated, nearly 20 years ago. I think it's safe to say that her outlook has changed. The point of sharing Sasha's story is actually to say that her experience of being left out happened before social media. She knew that 'cool plans' were happening without her; she knew that she was being excluded. But Sasha didn't have to deal with seeing it unfold in photo-documentation happening in real time. That hurts even more than just knowing. Talk about rubbing salt in a wound!

The trend of leaving people out and letting them know "has been especially steep among girls. 48 percent more girls said they often felt left out in 2015 than in 2010, compared with 27 percent more boys. Girls use social media more often, giving them additional opportunities to feel excluded and lonely when they see their friends or classmates getting together without them...

"These more dire consequences for teenage girls could also be rooted in the fact that they're more likely to experience cyberbullying. Boys tend to bully one another physically, while girls are more likely to do so by undermining a victim's

"My friends posted a Snapchat story about hanging out on a Saturday night. I wasn't invited and I felt really excluded." Marlene, 17

social status or relationships. Social media give middle and high school girls a platform on which to carry out the style of aggression they favor, ostracizing and excluding other girls around the clock."[14]

So, in other words, this magic way of staying in touch, this invention which is supposed to keep us connected...is actually making us feel more left out, and more alone.

Remember what Jennie said in Chapter Four: "Girls are just as aggressive as boys, just in different ways. Boys are physically aggressive, while girls mentally hurt each other."

Jennie's right. Online platforms give girls a stage to play out these mental games, and we are really good at them. The invention of social media has given us new tactics and tools and made our game even more hurtful.

"Social media companies are, of course, aware of these problems, and to one degree or another have endeavored to prevent cyberbullying. But their various motivations are, to say the least, complex. A recently leaked Facebook document indicated that the company had been touting to advertisers its ability to determine teens' emotional state based on their on-site behavior, and even to pinpoint 'moments when young people need a confidence boost.' Facebook acknowledged that the document was real, but denied that it offers 'tools to target people based on their emotional state.'"[15]

Wait, did I understand that correctly? Facebook is tempting advertisers by claiming that they know when young people need a "confidence boost?" In other words, companies are MAKING MONEY from my feeling bad about myself? YES. It happens all the time. Remember Chapter Two? Don't Question Yourself—Question the Media!

And all of this—being image obsessed, suffering from lowered self-esteem, comparing yourself to others, feeling left out— rests on the supreme power of the like. "Social media levy a psychic tax on the teen doing the posting as well, as she anxiously awaits the affirmation of comments and likes. When Athena [a young woman the author interviewed] posts pictures to Instagram, she told me, 'I'm nervous about what people think and are going to say. It sometimes bugs me when I don't get a certain amount of likes on a picture.'"[16] And don't forget where the like originated. Are you Hot or Not???????

## Remember the midriff?

In Chapter Two, we looked extensively at the ways in which the media teaches us to focus on our images. We saw that the media teaches us, in every way possible, that our bodies are our best assets. Remember the midriff? "Flaunt your sexuality, even if you don't understand it." Believe it or not, the video which taught us about the midriff—*The Merchants of Cool*—was made in 2001. Facebook was invented in 2004. Instagram in 2010. In other words, this image of the midriff, the over-sexualized girl, was ultra-popular before social media.

One might have thought that as soon as it became possible for us to create our own media, we'd do something more realistic. It would make sense that we would create media with images that actually look like us—that we would share realistic pictures and like photos that make us feel good. Right?

Nope, sorry.

Instead, we have created celebrities like the Kardashians, whose popularity is literally based on nothing more than their leveraging social media to become known...as sexual objects. We will get to the celebrity family in a minute, but for now I just want to point out how much we—women and girls—are playing into this dynamic of sexualization and objectification. In fact, I would argue that the invention of social media has made this dynamic worse.

"For many girls, the pressure to be considered 'hot' is felt on a nearly continual basis online. The sites with which they most commonly interact encourage them to post images of themselves, and employ the 'liking' feature, with which users can judge their appearance and, in effect, rate them. When girls post their pictures on Instagram or Snapchat or Facebook, they know they will be judged for their 'hotness,' and in a quantifiable way, with numbers of likes. Social media, which gave us selfies, seems to encourage an undue focus on appearance for everyone—but for girls, this focus is combined with a pervasive sexualization of girls in the wider culture, an overarching trend which is already having serious consequences."[17] In other words, many girls almost constantly feel a pressure to be hot—to be that dangerous combination of pretty and interesting...and sexy. And to show that sexiness to everyone else.

Peggy Orenstein, the author of *Girls and Sex: Navigating the Complicated New Landscape*, defines the idea of being hot as "a very narrow, commodified idea that tells girls over and over that how their bodies look to someone else matters more than how it feels to them."[18]

There is no denying it—girls are facing intense pressure to look sexy and act sexual. This pressure has existed for a long time, but the invention of social media has made it much more damaging for all the reasons I explained in this chapter, all the reasons social media impacts girls so deeply:

"I am affected by the types of pictures I see on social media. The types of pictures people, or actually women, post—where they look amazing, even if they are using filters and angles in order not to show how they look in reality—the virtual reality has an impact." Amit, 18

> We can't take a break from our phones, yet the more time we spend online the more unhappy we feel.

> We constantly compare ourselves to others via their profiles, and we forget that what we see online is only a very small part of a person's reality.

> We find ourselves left out of various social situations and we torment ourselves by watching them unfold in real time via photos and videos.

And, there's another issue: the pressure to be 'hot' not only comes from outside of us—from the media in particular—but also comes from within. We ourselves perpetuate this dynamic by objectifying ourselves online. WE are part of this culture of sexualization, and we feed it by posting sexualized photos of ourselves and liking those being posted by others.

A 2016 study called "Adolescent Self-Esteem and Instagram" looks at what teens choose to post and why. According to this research, boys and girls both believe "that girls place more emphasis than boys on selecting pictures in which they are attractive...The vast majority of girls posted profile photographs that presented them in a seductive manner (looking up or sideways at the viewer) and suggestive dress (showing cleavage)...There was a tendency for boys to choose photos that showed them at a farther distance from the camera and looking away from the viewer. However, there were also some boys who posed seductively, for example in photos that showed them shirtless.

"On one hand, these behaviors reproduce cultural gender stereotypes and media portrayals of the sexually available woman and the strong, emotionally distant man...On the other hand, the trend in the early 21st century for both boys and girls to self-sexualize in their visual online presentations suggests a more general phenomenon of 'self-commodification.'"[19] In other words, turning yourself into a commodity—a THING, rather than a person.

"Most of the time this is probably unconscious, as a result of internalization of media images...Young adults who internalized media messages about stereotypical looks were more likely to select profile photos in which they were posing seductively and revealingly dressed. The study participants displayed relatively high levels of media internalization overall, with females scoring significantly higher on the scale."[20]

In other words, on Facebook, Instagram and Snapchat, we replicate what we see in the media. And, to a large extent, what we see are sexualized women and distant men and, in turn, we post sexy pictures of ourselves. In some cases, we do this without even realizing it—and in others we do it intentionally. And sometimes, it's not clear. When a 12 year-old-girl posts a seductive picture, is she aware of what she is doing?

I am pointing out our role in this dynamic—as those who are taking and posting sexy photos of ourselves and liking and encouraging those of others—so that we can both see how this behavior impacts our well-being as well as empower ourselves to take control of it. I fully recognize that it can be really challenging to stand up to the social pressures on us to look/act/be sexual.

I also understand that by claiming our part in this culture of objectification, by recognizing that we sometimes contribute to it, rather than reject it, we empower ourselves to make good choices.

## The Kardashian effect

Sadly, no reflection on the influence of social media on teens would be complete without at least a reference to the Kardashians, the family who has risen to fame for—well, basically, nothing. Leading the pack is Kim, often referred to as the 'selfie queen,' especially since the 2015 publication of her book *Selfish*—a compilation of selfies. She's become famous through a mastery of using social media to promote herself.

She's not a talented actress, or a musician, she hasn't written poetry that will inspire us, she's not famous for playing sports or for her role in politics. She's famous for taking selfies.

"The Kardashian lifestyle was the fulfillment of a new American dream which had been embraced by many girls and young women, unsurprisingly enough, at a time when everything around them supported it as an ideal: it was to be beautiful, famous, rich, have amazing clothes, bags and shoes and tens of millions of followers on social media. It was to get tens or even hundreds of thousands of likes on all your selfies."[21]

At the writing of this chapter in late 2018, Kim has 120 million followers on Instagram (and this number is constantly skyrocketing) and her photos literally get thousands of comments. Some pics have over a million likes. That seems to be the definition of popularity in the age of social media.

But the thing that gets me, above all else, is that so many of Kim's selfies are ultra, ultra sexual. "Kim used the technological tools now available to almost everyone to get what everyone wanted. What she'd been doing relentlessly since the introduction of smartphones and before, now everybody was doing—using social media to self-promote, to craft an idealized online self. And girls coming of age in the second decade of the 21st century are using it to present a sexualized self.

"My little cousin, she's 13, and she posts such inappropriate pictures on Instagram and boys post sexual comments, and she's like, 'thank you.' It's child porn, and everyone's looking at it on their iPhones in the cafeteria," said a 17-year-old girl in New York."[22]

So it's not just that taking and posting pictures of ourselves has become totally normal (remember what Nancy Jo Sales said about how, "On social media, things which once might have been considered outrageous or disturbing come to seem normal very quickly through widespread repetition."[23]) It's that taking super sexualized pictures has become the new normal. Turning ourselves into a brand—a thing to be attained—has become the new normal.

Many teens are creating a self—basically a brand—that they are promoting on social media. This is similar to what I said earlier about the concept of showing only certain aspects of our lives—but much more extreme.

And for something to be a brand—rather than a person—we need to turn it into an image, an idea...an object.

How do things get branded? Sexualize them. Remember what Nicole said in Chapter Two—"Sex sells."

It's not just that we are using social media—a lot. And it's not just that our emotions are deeply affected by the media we consume, what we see on other people's profiles, or how many likes we get. The real clincher is that those likes—for girls, much, much more than for boys—are connected to our hotness. In other words, to be popular, like Kim Kardashian and many others like her, we are willing to turn ourselves into a brand, a sexualized brand—and in doing so, we are basically creating pornographic images...of ourselves.

I understand that it can be empowering to take and post photos that express our sexuality. It is empowering to express our sexuality and it is completely natural to do so, and important for us to have such opportunities.

But I wonder, is the way in which we are expressing our sexuality online—as something that can be commodified, as something for just anyone to comment on—healthy? Is this kind of expression supporting our development as young women? Is it helping us cultivate sexual relationships that are meaningful and mutually respectful? Or is this online free-for-all cheapening something which is actually very personal and sacred? Turning ourselves into a brand and emphasizing our appearance, especially our sexualized appearance, above all, reduces us to something so much more superficial than who we actually are. Is that really how you want others to see you? And, more importantly, how does this kind of portrayal—objectifying and sexualizing yourself—affect YOU? How does it actually make you feel?

I can't help but feel that there is something in this phenomenon that completely undermines us, that completely takes away our personal power as women and as sexual beings. The issue is less about posting sexy pics—and more about why we are posting them. The problem is that we aren't just expressing our sexuality—we're doing something else: we are posting photos to appeal to others, often without thinking about how it affects us.

Ask yourself:
> Why are you posting these photos?
> Are you posting a sexy photo because expressing your sexuality in this way makes you feel good?

## Social media and sexual harassment

When I was a teenager, looking at porn meant that maybe someone got their hands on a magazine, a magazine whose photos showed naked women, probably altered in some way, and generally looking not that real. I don't remember having a feeling that I wanted to look like any of those women. Today, porn is all over—I am not just talking about movies or images that are explicitly defined as pornographic, but rather pointing out that ads, TV, movies, even our own social media profiles contain very sexualized images, especially of women. These images are so widespread that we have come to accept them as normal. This new normal has a deep, devastating impact on the way we see ourselves as women, and of course, how men and boys see us and what they expect from us.

Culture has impacted what is considered accepted behavior. As it has become more accepted to sexualize and objectify women in photos, it has also become more accepted to do so in real life. There is a connection between the proliferation of sexual images online and the pervasiveness of sexual harassment. There is a connection between the proliferation of sexual images online and the acceptance of disrespectful, and even violent behavior towards women. Again, if we accept seeing women as objects, it also becomes acceptable to treat women as objects. That being said, the way I treat someone is MY OWN responsibility to manage. It's really important for me to emphasize that I AM NOT SAYING that any woman is at fault if she is sexually harassed.

It would take another entire book (or a few) to adequately give this topic the space it deserves. But I am raising this issue here to point out how social media has impacted the way women are treated. It's a very serious issue that we desperately need

**Think about it**

> Do you really feel that the way you portray yourself online is a true reflection of you?

> Are you performing or changing yourself to get attention? Is it the attention you want?

> How does the way you portray yourself online make you feel?

to work on fixing. I deeply believe that WE—you, too!—can improve our problematic culture if we take this situation into our own hands.

As we become more aware of the way we present ourselves, in real life and online, we can change how we feel, particularly when we consciously choose to present ourselves in the way we want to be seen. In our actions and our attitudes, we can RE-EDUCATE those around us and redefine our culture.

**What can I do about it?**

Wow. After reading all that, it would be really easy to say that social media is evil, it hurts girls in particular, it makes us more lonely, more sexualized, more depressed...

It would also be easy to just give up and say that social media has taken over our culture and that there is nothing that I—one individual person—can do. Not true. I can change the way I see this phenomenon; I can change the way I use and interact with social media, and in doing so I can help us, as a culture, define what healthy use of social media looks like.

I KNOW that you can define the way you use these media, and you can determine what impact you want them to have on you.

I want to remind you that social media is a gift in many respects. There are some really great ways to get support online. I have had countless students whose coming out processes were deeply influenced by people they met via social media or relevant websites. I have had students whose first steps toward getting help and advice they needed came from online sources, especially when they were embarrassed to ask people in real life. I've worked with teens coming from very sheltered communities whose discovery of information online helped them forge their own paths, sometimes learning things their parents were not teaching them.

There are also people who post to share about the death of a loved one and find support from their online communities. Social media is a very efficient way to share something with many people, especially when it is something difficult to repeat over and over, but it's really important to be aware that getting a message from someone offering support is very different from getting a hug or being able to cry with a friend.

\*\*\*

So basically, my approach to social media is the same as my attitude about teens and sex, drugs or drinking: I am not going to tell you NOT to use Instagram or Snapchat or whatever else. That would be silly, because if I say that then I lose the opportunity to actually talk to you about the issue—whether it's social media, having a drink, or doing something sexual. I accept the reality that these technologies have become a very, very significant part of our lives. And I understand that it's completely up to us to determine whether they have a positive or negative impact on us. How do we determine that?

\*\*\*

To learn more about how we can develop the skills to successfully manage our use of social media, I interviewed Dr. Robin Stern, a psychologist who specializes in emotional intelligence and has a great deal of experience around issues connected to social media. She said, "Awareness is the first step towards doing anything. If you go on social media and it makes you feel hot and popular, you aren't going to want to change."[24] It's really important to keep track of how you feel—in general—in order to understand how different things we do impact our moods. Once we know how we feel, we can respond in a way that makes sense. So, check yourself: is using social media actually making you happy?

There are many great benefits to these technologies. In order to enjoy the benefits, we need to be aware of the real impact the technology is having on us.

***

Dr. Stern suggests **tracking your social media use**—do you know how much time you actually spend online? Is that amount of time really right for you? Often we can think we only spend an hour a day, for example, but then when we really take a week and write down each time we check something on a profile or post, those few seconds here and there, all day, really add up.

***

She also suggests **tracking your mood**—how does checking your Instagram actually make you feel? Write yourself some quick notes each time you finish a session on social media so that you can really be aware of how your mood is affected. The Center for Emotional Intelligence at Yale University (Dr. Stern is the Associate Director) developed an app called the Mood Meter™ which literally helps the user keep track of how s/he is feeling. Check it out. Try to name your feelings as clearly as possible so that you can later have useful information to support your own growth. For example, for some people, going online helps them feel connected to other people, while others feel more lonely when they spend time on the Internet.

Dr. Stern emphasizes that **once you know how you really feel, you will figure out how to deal with the feeling you are facing**. (This is, of course, true in many situations, not just with regard to social media.) "If you notice that you want something that you actually don't have and other people have it, you can set your course to understand what is keeping you from it and how you can get it."[25] This way, instead of feeling jealous and unhappy about it, you can really be clear: I feel jealous of _____ because she has _____. Then you can decide: if I really want what she has too, what steps do I need to take to get there? Or, you might realize that you don't actually care that much about the thing that seemed to make you feel jealous and then you can let go of the feeling.

***

The same can be true if you feel excluded from something that you saw pictures of—did you really want to go to that event? Why weren't you there? If it is because you weren't invited, think carefully about whether you actually want to be friends with people who are purposefully leaving you out. How did finding out that you were excluded make you feel? Were you hurt? Sad? Angry? Have you felt these feelings before in relation to the same people? Take the moment as an opportunity to think twice about the people behind it all and decide what is truly best for you and your well-being.

In general, this raises the issue of boundaries and limits. We know how important it is to set boundaries in our relationships—to tell someone when something doesn't work for us, to know when we feel uncomfortable in a situation and need to change it. We also need to set boundaries for ourselves with regard to our use of our phones and social media. This is true for **everyone** right now, adults and teens alike. As a culture, we are addicted to our phones and each of us needs to take responsibility for our relationship with technology. No doubt.

***

That being said, I fully recognize that many young people feel like they have to be on social media, and check frequently in order to keep up with their social scene. Even so, I still think that we can **set healthy limits for ourselves**. Think about it: do you have clear limits and boundaries in your life in general? Are your parents good at setting limits for you? Some teens might say that their parents are way too strict and have too many rules. Others might say that their parents give them so much freedom that it can be overwhelming. Others still might be aware that the limits being set for them are always changeable, that when they are told they can be on the phone for an hour, it will be really easy to convince mom to just let it go after that hour is up. The modeling we get from the adults around us impacts the way we set boundaries for ourselves. It is really useful and important to be able to set limits and stick to them. If our parents aren't able to help us do this, we need to do it ourselves.

If you are the kid whose parents are on their phones constantly, Dr. Stern suggests, you can take the opportunity to lead in your own family. Ask everyone to agree not to use their phones at dinner, for example. You can do the same among your friends. I love the idea of 'stacking'—if I go out to a meal with a group of people, we all stack our phones on the table and agree not to use them. The first person to break the pact and touch her phone has to buy dinner for everyone. I didn't come up with this idea, but I think it is a GREAT way to be aware of our impulsive use of our phones and how much that can take us away from actual, live interactions with others. Lead by example by being aware of how much you are on your phone and setting limits for yourself. Your behavior will impact those around you.

*** 

**Pause before you post**. Take a second to ask yourself—is this really what I want to share? It's so simple to post or share online that it's become almost automatic. How many times have you seen something incredible and right away, before you have even had a moment to take it in, it's captured on your phone and reached hundreds of friends? Give yourself the chance to think twice.

Think about it:
> How do I choose what to post and why?
> Do I even have a sense of the potential impact of a post about myself or someone else?

I am sure people have told you about how what goes on your profile stays there forever, later in life employers might see that photo of you at a party...this is true. And I also understand that it doesn't really take on so much importance in your thinking, which is often very much about what is happening right now. But even so, thinking twice before I post gives me the chance to give a second thought about the right now—do I really want that picture to be seen by my whole school? Is this a comment that I want to write?

***

And certainly, think twice before you share something that makes someone else look bad. Photos can go viral in seconds, and we've all seen it happen. I never want to be the girl sitting in class as everyone's phones are buzzing around me, and each time one does, the owner looks at it, makes a face and looks at me. And then she shares. And who knows how many more people will see that compromising photo of me. Those kinds of scenarios happen ALL THE TIME. **Be sensitive about what you share**. And if it's your picture being shared, respond. That's harassment, and you don't need to stand for it.

When you share something about yourself, really think—does this reflect who I really am? Try to **stay in touch with your true self**, even when you are online. Be mindful of the influence of our culture, encouraging us to be obsessed with an image and to try to be that image, encouraging us to value our appearance more and more, and give less and less regard to our internal, true self.

***

**Spend time, in person, with people you love**. It can be really easy to feel like we are cultivating meaningful relationships online, when we are messaging all the time and feel constantly updated about things going on in other people's lives. But knowing what someone ate for lunch or where they were yesterday isn't enough to build real closeness. Meaningful friendships grow out of really getting to know one another, sharing experiences and building trust. While this can happen through online channels, there is no replacement for hanging out in person.

***

**Make sure you have enough time with the people you want around you.** All in all, remember, **social media is only part of your social life**, which is made up of many important relationships, and lots of different types of interactions.

# SEVEN

# Sex—AHHHHHHHH!

I am not going to tell you what to do when it comes to sex. You are your own person, and you are going to make your own decisions about what you do with your body. And that's the way it should be. No one else can determine what happens to your body.

I don't believe you take it seriously when adults say that you shouldn't do anything sexual. Why should you? I understand the reality. Sexual experiences can be beautiful and meaningful; they can help us connect to our bodies and to our partners in really personal and intimate ways. In the right moment, with the right person, sexual exploration can be wonderful. This is what we all deserve—to enjoy sexual experiences that make us feel good, both about ourselves and about our interactions with others.

Sex is a really basic part of our culture and it affects many aspects of our lives. It's difficult to go online or watch TV without seeing something sexually suggestive. We've discussed this at great length in the chapter about being thought of as an object (Chapter Two), and I don't need to repeat everything we discussed there. All I will say is that we get really confusing messages about sex from the world around us. We see women everywhere using their sexuality as a tool to get power, to sell products, or to attract attention.

We're taught that our sexual prowess and beauty can get us anything we want—*if* we are willing to exploit or take advantage of them. That *if*—the exploitation part—really complicates things. Sex is personal and private; by listening to your inner voice, you will find your own way to express yourself sexually when you are are ready.

### Sex = communication

Sexual behavior is a form of communication, only it is different from simply talking. It's more like shaking hands, in that people are communicating with their bodies. There can be direct talking involved, but lots of sexual behavior is about touching. Our bodies can be stimulated by many different things, and what turns you on is entirely personal. There is no specific 'normal' thing that should arouse you, but know that it is totally normal to feel aroused, and you are not weird if you experience that feeling, or if you don't.

### Some things that might make people feel aroused

• Thinking about someone you like • Seeing someone you like • Touching someone you like (could be simply holding hands, or even brushing your skin on their skin, or intentionally touching or rubbing intimate places) • Touching yourself intimately

# What exactly does 'having sex' mean?

## Using Your Mouth

> **Kissing**: This can be simply giving a quick peck on the cheek or on the lips, or it could be longer, keeping your lips pressed to someone else's, maybe opening your mouths and feeling your tongue playing with someone else's. People might kiss each other all over, or use their tongues on their partner's body, to turn them on. Even though kissing is the first thing lots of people do with sexual partners, kissing can be much more intimate and personal than other activities.

> **Going Down**: This generally refers to oral sex, and involves using the mouth or tongue to stimulate your partner's genitals. Some people call this 'eating out,' 'giving head,' or giving someone a 'blow job.'

## Using Your Hands

> **Touching**: This is a really big part of sexual arousal, and some areas are more sensitive than others. Being touched on your breasts or genitals is likely to turn you on; touching on your lips, hands, neck, thighs, and back can be equally exciting. Some people like to feel their partner's skin against them anywhere.

> **Feeling Up**: Touching a woman's breasts/nipples with your hands

> **Hand Job**: Using your hands to stimulate a man's penis

> **Fingering**: Touching a woman's genitals, either on the outside (rubbing her clitoris) or on the inside (by inserting fingers into her vagina)

## Using Your Genitals

> **Doing It, Having Sex, Making Love**: These often refer to vaginal sex.*

> **Anal Sex**: Inserting the penis into the anus

Most important, remember that sexual experiences are an opportunity for you to enjoy yourself and enjoy the sensations in your body.

*A note about sexual intercourse: Lots of people think that vaginal sex is the main event when it comes to sexual behavior, and there is a lot of pressure to do this particular act. For some women, foreplay (the stuff you do leading up to sex) is just as exciting as actually having sex, if not more so. And it's always important to remember that vaginal sex with a man is the act that can lead to pregnancy. If you don't feel ready to deal with this possibility, there are still many other things you can do to enjoy your sexuality.

## Owning your sexuality

More than anything, I want you to understand that decisions about what you do with your body are YOUR DECISIONS. Your sexuality is exactly that—yours—to enjoy and explore in the situations and ways that you choose.

When I think back on my experiences, I wish that I had been able to listen to myself. My colleague, Tohar Lauffer-Zeevi, wrote the following when she began to work with girls. The messages she shares have become the basis for her communication with girls in conversations about sexuality. I too wish I had heard these messages when I was a teenager. Tohar really sums it up; I think her words are relevant for all of us in our ongoing expression of our sexuality, no matter how old we are.

# Messages about my sexuality I wish I'd heard as a teenager

> Your body is your temple. Enjoy it as much as possible. Be aware of what you like and what you want. And know how to express that.

> Your passion is your gift. Explore your body because you want to, when you feel it is good for you. Sexuality has infinite expressions. There is no one way to explore it.

> Don't allow the images you see in the media to shape your idea of sexuality. Teach yourself and your partner, slowly, as if neither of you has ever heard about sex, as if you are inventing it all. Allow yourself to approach sexuality with a fresh start, without any prejudices or goals.

> Don't compromise. Ever. You deserve the BEST.

> Remember to be present. Try not to allow expectations to guide you. A good sexual encounter is not a fantasy—it's real, here and now.

> Bring all of yourself to your sexuality, without giving up on any part of yourself. Know that your pleasure is your partner's pleasure. Only what is good for you can actually be good for your partner.

> Don't be afraid of your desires or your passions. They are yours and they serve you well.

> If you know how to say 'yes' about what you like, the ability to say 'no' will come naturally when you need it to. Listening to yourself is what will allow you to understand your boundaries. The sky's the limit. As you connect with your own unique sexual expression, you will discover a whole new world.

> Your sexuality is your gift—whether you choose to share it with someone else or not. Sensuality is the discovery of the pleasure of your senses. Allow all of your senses to take part. Let yourself dance— express your true beauty.

> There are no stages in sex. There is no one thing that leads to another. Nothing is determined in advance. Don't ever push yourself into something that doesn't come naturally, even if it seems like something should be the 'next step.'

> When it comes to sex, there is no place for comparison. There is no 'good' or 'not good.' It's only a matter of being more or less connected to yourself. When you are sexual, you are the only woman in the world. Your role is to be yourself and no one can do that better than you.

> Enjoy yourself!

Tohar, 21

"I'm not one to just hook up with anybody. It has got to mean something. I am also stuck on the whole fairy tale idea of having sex with someone you love. My first time is reserved for my first love, and if that means I have to wait a little bit, then that is what I will do. I want to have fond memories and no regrets. I don't expect the guy I lose my virginity with to be my husband. I just expect him to love and care for me at that specific moment in time. I'm taking my life one step at a time, and right now sex is not a part of it." Dana, 17

## Making sexual decisions

Asking yourself these questions can really help you listen to your own inner voice when you are making a decision about something sexual:

> Is this fun for me?

> Do I feel ready for this?

> Do I feel comfortable in this situation?

> Does this feel good in my body?

> Am I enjoying myself?

"Being sexual is fun and exciting! My boyfriend and I have learned how and where to touch each other to really make the other person excited. We're exploring each other's bodies, and bonding in the process. I've been with other guys before, but no one has made me feel as good as he does. I'm not ready for full on intercourse yet, but we are having lots of fun just playing around." Anna, 19

I remember, when I was in 8th grade, there was a heated conversation going on in our class and one boy blurted out, "Is sex fun?" We were all shocked by how bold he was and even more surprised when the teacher banged her fists on the desk, stood up and screamed "YES!" I had never heard this message before from an adult.

It is so important to share that message—that, first and foremost, sexual experiences are to be enjoyed. From the basis of that understanding, you can explore and discover in the ways that are right for you. Having fun, positive sexual experiences means listening to myself, and understanding and expressing what makes me feel good. In a sexual encounter with someone else, share what is working for you, and what isn't. Sometimes our partners will understand what we want from our body language; sometimes we need to use words to make ourselves clear. If you find yourself in a situation where you need to say something that is hard to express, you can always take a break for a second, go to the bathroom and let the energy shift so that you can find your center again.

Remember: You never owe anyone anything. You are never obligated to do something to or for someone else if you don't want to.

**Sex and peer pressure**

Sex and peer pressure are really closely linked. Just like the media seems to set the standard for how we should look, and pressures us and our peers to fit that standard, it also sets the standard for how we should behave. Media messages tell us to flaunt our sexuality; we think that we will be more popular if we act like the people we see online or on TV, even if we have no interest in doing anything sexual just yet. At the same time, we also get the message that we should be 'pure' and will be considered 'sluts' if we are sexual.

I've done things with guys lots of times when there was nothing romantic about the interaction. I let myself get involved in situations that weren't right for me or because I thought that was what I was supposed to do. I thought 'getting with guys' would make me more popular, happier, or feel better about myself. And so I did, without really thinking about respecting myself. I didn't know how to listen to my inner voice when it came to being sexual, or maybe I didn't even realize that voice existed. I was really affected by the pressure to 'have sexual experiences.' I didn't have an older sister or anyone whom I was really comfortable talking to about sex, so I felt alone as I tried to figure out what to do. I also didn't understand that it was okay for me to say no if I didn't want to do something.

Once, in high school, this kid named Evan who I knew from my Spanish class—and didn't really like—asked me to kiss him. We were at a party, and there were a lot of other kids from our school there. I gave him a quick peck on the cheek and turned away, embarrassed, because I could see that there were people watching us. He was much more popular than I was, and I thought that even though it was embarrassing, kissing this boy would help make me more popular. He responded by telling me he wanted a "real kiss." I really didn't want to do it, but next thing I knew I had this guy's tongue in my mouth. I let it happen, but felt pretty dirty about the whole thing.

"It was the night before Halloween, and there was a big costume party at this senior girl's house. There was a keg of beer. I hadn't been introduced to the party scene before, but now I was hanging out with this new group of girls. There was all this talk about getting with guys. I had never hooked up with anyone before. All the girls I was with had. The idea of hooking up with random people for only one night was brand new to me. We were all drunk and having a good time. The cops came, so two girlfriends and I got a ride with three guys (one of whom was sober). We were looking for another party to go to. One of the boys in the car was showing interest in me. Boys hadn't shown interest in me before. Maybe he was interested because I was a new addition to this group of girls who are known for hooking up with people. I felt really uncomfortable, and I realized that I wasn't one of those girls, and that random hookups weren't for me. I wasn't with people I trusted. Everyone else got out of the car, and I felt really pressured to hook up with this guy. I knew I didn't want to do it, but I really wanted to fit in with this group of girls. I hooked up with him, and ended up feeling dirty and just kind of like the typical girl who conforms to the people around her to be a part of the popular party scene.

"I came home that night wishing I never went out. When I see that guy at school, I feel so little. I've grown up a lot since then and don't identify with those girls. I really thought about what happened, about who I want to be and how I want to be seen by my peers. I don't want to be seen as easy or fast, because I am not that girl. Nothing like that has happened since, and it won't ever happen again. In high school you are really judged by things you do with other people—by who you hook up with. I don't like hook-ups. For me, they are just not pleasing at all." Camilla, 16

I think that if I had felt more secure about myself, I wouldn't have let that scene with Evan go down the way it did. I would have been able to recognize that I wasn't comfortable with the situation, and that I didn't have to stick around if I didn't want to. It is really important for us to recognize that, even though sex is such a big part of our culture and seems so public, the decisions we make about our bodies are actually really personal and private.

Sexual activities are fun and exciting only when you are a willing participant, or, in other words, you are in full agreement with what is happening. This means really saying yes, in your heart, head and body, in the moment, to whatever is going on. This can sometimes be confusing because maybe you enjoyed something last week and this week you aren't into it, or maybe it's clear to you that you like the person you are with, but in the moment something just doesn't feel right. Sexuality is dynamic, and it's okay if your feelings change. Just because you enjoyed something in the past, doesn't mean you have to do it again if you don't want to. Even if you have already done it before with this particular person—our needs and desires change, and it is important to communicate our feelings in order to manifest positive sexual experiences for ourselves and our partners.

## Unwelcome sex

"It was the last day of eighth grade. In two and a half months, I'd be entering the new and chaotic world of high school. But for now, it was summer and all my friends and I wanted to do was celebrate the end of junior high school.

"Kiera was throwing a party that night. I had never been to a house party before, and I was extremely excited. It was going to be my excuse to let loose and dance the night—and middle school—away.

"The four of us arrived at the party feeling stylish and ready to make an entrance. Walking up the stairs, dark rooms full of people lay in front of me. I entered the first room, ready to make it over to the group of girls dancing, when I felt a hand firmly plant [itself] on my right butt cheek and squeeze. I turned around, only to see a bunch of anonymous bodies, just dark figures.

"My excitement and party mood quickly came to a halt, and I plopped down on a bench near the door. The next thing I knew, a boy had taken my legs up in the air, wrapped them around his shoulders, and started grinding on me. I pushed him off in disgust. I resorted to the front porch. I sat down on a step for the rest of the night.

If I was sitting, no one would be able to grab my ass, and if I was outside, away from the music, random drunk boys wouldn't start grinding on me.

"For the rest of the night, I beat myself up. Why didn't I turn on the light and slap someone? Why didn't I put that boy in his place? I have to let them know that's not okay! But the truth is, I was scared.

"That night, I learned what it is like to feel vulnerable. I put up a guard, sort of a shield, which probably won't ever come down." **Cara, 16**

Unfortunately, there are lots of situations in which girls get pressured into doing things they don't want to do. Situations like these are really uncomfortable, and you shouldn't have to tolerate them. If you find yourself in any of these situations, talk to someone you trust. Being forced into sexual behavior shouldn't be taken lightly. There is no reason to be ashamed if something like this happens to you—it's not your fault. Keeping your story inside can make you feel alone in dealing with it. Sharing with someone else can be a great support.

Unwelcome sex might include any of
the following:

> **Sexual Harassment**—when someone
talks to you in a way that makes you
uncomfortable, or tells you that they will
do something for you if you do something
sexual with them. This might happen in
person, on the phone, or online. The person
harassing you might be your friend, a
family member, or an authority figure. No
matter who is doing it, sexual harassment
is NOT OKAY.

> **Sexual Assault**—when someone does
something to you that you don't want. This
might mean unwelcome touching, forced
kissing, or any other physical contact that
you don't agree to. Again, no matter who is
assaulting you, this behavior is NOT OKAY.

> **Rape**—when someone pushes
themselves on you, and tries to force you
to have sex. Rape is a serious crime. If you
are raped, find help immediately. It's really
overwhelming to deal with these kinds
of traumatic situations alone. Sometimes
girls are raped by people they know. This is
often referred to as 'date rape.' Even if the
person who forced you into sex is someone
you know, that still does not make it okay.
Date rape is still rape, even if a person you
like or have a crush on does it.

## A word about porn

The invention of the Internet has made it really, really easy to access pornography. This access, combined with the natural curiosity we experience about sex and the lack of quality sex education in our culture, has led to many teenagers to turn to porn for answers.

Peggy Orenstein, the author of *Girls and Sex: Navigating the Complicated New Landscape*, shares that in the three years she spent interviewing young women in high school and college for her book, she heard, again and again, that young people are searching for answers by watching porn. A 21-year-old woman wrote to her, "'there's a lot of problems with porn...but it is kind of nice to be able to use it to gain some knowledge of sex.'

"According to a survey of college students in Britain, 60 percent consult pornography, at least in part, as though it were an instruction manual, even as nearly three-quarters say that they know it is as realistic as pro wrestling."[1]

Younger teens tend to see porn as more realistic. In a study of young people aged 11 to 16, 53 percent of boys and 39 percent of girls saw pornography as a realistic depiction of sex.

Some thoughts from the students who participated in the study:

> "One of my friends has started treating women like he sees on the videos—not major—just a slap here or there." (13-year-old boy)
> "It can make a boy not look for love, just look for sex, and it can pressure us girls to act and look and behave in a certain way before we might be ready for it." (13-year-old girl)
> "A few of my friends have used it for guidance about sex and are getting the wrong image of relationships." (13-year-old girl)[2]

While there is so much to say about this topic, I want to emphasize one very important point: So much of sexual expression among teens—and adults—is deeply impacted by the prevalence of pornography. Pornography is a performance. Sex is not. The way sex is depicted in porn is so, so unrealistic and confuses acting 'sexy' with being 'sexual.' Acting sexy is just that—acting; being sexual is about physically and emotionally exploring your sexuality in the various ways described in this chapter or in whatever way you personally choose. [3] In addition, pornographic images often teach us that sex is about pleasuring men, and that sexual encounters reach their peak (and often end) when the man ejaculates. This is simply not true. A great deal of research demonstrates that women who have sex with women report enjoying sex much more than women who have sex with men. Women who have sex with men deserve to enjoy themselves just as much as their partners. I can't emphasize this enough—explore for your own pleasure! Don't let media images of sex define how you explore—especially when so much of what the media shows is about men's enjoyment.

YOU are the person who decides about your body. Be aware of the impact pornography has on young people's perceptions of sex and sexuality. Do what feels good for you, no matter what you or your partner think you are 'supposed to do' or how you think sex is 'supposed to look.' Be true to yourself and pursue your pleasure.

**How can we respond to the pressures around us?**

First of all, it's really important to understand that our society is full of mixed messages about sex. On one hand, sex is all over the media and very present in the world around us. Lots of people dress very suggestively, and act sexy. On the other hand, adults aren't often open to talking about sex in a way that gives kids a realistic understanding of what sex and sexuality are about. Many schools have sex education, but most schools don't distribute condoms, and are really wary about doing anything that might seem like it is encouraging kids to have sex. But the reality is that kids are naturally curious about sex—that curiosity is actually an animal instinct—and it is important to know that it is normal to feel that way. At some point, you might want to know more about what kissing, touching, and generally being sexual is like. Again, that curiosity is totally normal, and even though we don't tend to talk openly about sex in our society, it's normal for you to want to try things out, to want to experiment with other people or by yourself.

## Masturbation (touching yourself sexually)

Have you ever heard anyone say:

> "People who masturbate are dirty."

> "Masturbation is for people who can't get a boyfriend/girlfriend."

> "Masturbation is bad for you."

None of these is true. There is nothing wrong with acting on sexual feelings on your own. Masturbating can help you learn what feels good to you, and what doesn't. There is nothing dangerous about masturbating (as long as you are not touching yourself with something unclean or sharp). You can masturbate by yourself or with a partner. Whatever feels good to you is the right thing to do.

Experimenting on your own is a great idea; you can feel some of the physical aspects of being sexual without the pressure of being with someone else. No matter what anyone else tells you, masturbation is normal; many, many people do it—boys and girls—and there's nothing dirty about it.

It's also normal to be curious about experimenting with other girls. You might decide to define yourself as bisexual because you are interested in both girls and boys, or as a lesbian because you are more interested in girls than you are in boys, but that is your choice, and comes from what you feel in your heart. You don't need to give a name to your sexual exploration if you don't want to.

"Going into high school I was very nervous about boys and wasn't very experienced. I was scared because I never really had anyone to talk to that had been intimate with a boy, and didn't know what to expect. A way for guys not to like me and want to be with me was being overweight. I would gain weight in order for boys not to like me." Dana, 16

"First kisses are the best. They are my favorite thing. When you have been waiting to kiss each other for so long and you both know it and then you finally do, it's like bliss." Celia, 16

It is also important to understand that it is totally normal not to feel interested in sex or kissing or anything sexual at all. The pressure we feel to be sexual is overwhelming, and I think it distorts our own personal timelines for being ready to enjoy sex.

I know it seems impossible that it can be normal to be interested and normal not to be interested, but it really is. There is no 'right time' to be doing anything. This is entirely up to you to decide. Your peers, your parents, your environment, your culture, your religion, and lots of other factors will influence your decision. As difficult as it is, though, I think it is really important to feel, for yourself, whether you are comfortable doing whatever you might be considering, and equally important, to feel whether you are comfortable talking with your partner about whatever you might be doing. The rule I like to encourage my students to follow is: IF YOU CAN'T TALK ABOUT IT, YOU PROBABLY SHOULDN'T BE DOING IT.

## Being aware

There are some physical risks associated with sexual behavior, and it's important to know what they are. When you are intimate with someone, you are putting yourself at risk of contracting certain diseases. You need to know where your partner has been, and if you plan on getting intimate, you should both get tested for STDs (Sexually Transmitted Diseases). Needless to say, if you are having vaginal sex with a man, pregnancy is a possibility. Think carefully about what might change in your life if you were to have a baby. Are you prepared to talk to your partner about these risks? Will you be partners in handling any tough situation that might arise?

## What can lead to what?[4]

> Kissing on the mouth (French kissing) puts you at risk of getting a cold, the flu or Hepatitis B. Cut the risk by getting the Hepatitis B vaccine and not kissing someone who is sick.

> Mutual masturbation (includes fingering and hand jobs) isn't risky, as long as you have no cuts on your hands or genitals. If you do have cuts on your hands or genitals and you do this with someone who has HIV, you're at risk if infected sperm or vaginal fluid enters your bloodstream. Cut the risk by using a barrier, like latex.

> Oral sex (on a man or woman) puts you at risk of contracting Herpes, HIV, Hepatitis B, Gonorrhea, Syphilis and genital warts. Cut the risk by using a condom (on a man) or a dental dam (on a woman).

> Vaginal sex puts you at risk of pregnancy, as well as of contracting Herpes, HIV, Hepatitis B, Gonorrhea, Syphilis, Chlamydia, genital warts and crabs. Cut the risk by using a condom (male or female).

> Anal sex puts you at risk of contracting Herpes, HIV, Hepatitis B, Gonorrhea, Syphilis, Chlamydia and genital warts. Cut the risk by using a condom.

## A word about pregnancy

Remember, the biological reason we engage in sex is to reproduce. Female bodies are designed to have babies, and we are trying to beat nature by having sex with men without getting pregnant. The only way to be 100 percent sure that you will not become pregnant is not to have sex at all.

Pregnancy happens when a sperm makes its way into your vagina and through your fallopian tubes, where it meets and penetrates an egg. The meeting of sperm and egg is called fertilization. Once a fertilized egg implants into the wall of your uterus, you are pregnant.

Using a condom (or taking the pill or using another form of birth control) decreases the risk of pregnancy. To learn more about what birth control methods are appropriate for you, talk to your doctor. If you think you might be pregnant, talk to your doctor to test for pregnancy, and to discuss the options available to you. If you are pregnant and feel comfortable with your partner, talk to him about deciding together what you will do.

## Always remember

**Know what is going on in your body**. If you are sexually active, go to the gynecologist regularly (at least once a year) for checkups. Tell your doctor that you are sexually active, and ask him/her to test you for STDs. Ask him/her to talk to you about safe sex and ask for advice about how to take care of yourself. Your doctor is required to keep this information confidential. If you don't have a regular doctor, go to Planned Parenthood or another clinic in your area. Call 1-800-230-PLAN (1-800-230-7526) or go to www.plannedparenthood.org to find the clinic nearest to you.

**Don't mix sex with alcohol or drugs**. I will talk about this more in the next chapter, but I just want you to keep in mind that alcohol and drugs change your state of consciousness and make it difficult to make clear decisions. You don't need drugs or alcohol to enjoy being sexual.

**Talk to your partner about both of your sexual histories**. It's better to be honest and safe now than to be sorry later. Communication will only bring you closer together.

I know it can seem like the risks associated with sexual behaviors take away the fun. They don't. Having the information is important so that you can take care of your health.

**Enjoy!**

Above all, remember that sexual activity is an animal instinct and an emotional desire that our bodies and brains are designed to enjoy. We are built to want to have sex so that we will reproduce and continue our species. People want to have sex and engage in sexual behaviors because, when we are comfortable, these behaviors are fun. Feeling safe with someone you care about is a positive experience. When you are ready, sexual experimentation can be an extremely enjoyable experience that makes both you and your partner feel great.

"I am in a serious relationship now, my first one ever. I lost my virginity to my now boyfriend. He was really careful and kind and gentle. Every time I had a look on my face that didn't look like I was enjoying myself, he asked me, 'Are you sure? Should I keep going? Am I hurting you?' It was really open and honest, and we communicated about everything. The best thing I kept hearing him say was, 'I'll stop if you want.' I didn't want him to stop, but hearing a boy say that is a big relief.

"At first I didn't tell my mom, but after a few weeks, I did, and she has been really cool about the whole thing. It felt really good to tell her, and that way I know that if anything were to go wrong, if something came up, there wouldn't be a whole fiasco about telling her. I wouldn't have to say, 'Mom, the condom broke and oh, by the way, I am sexually active.' I could just tell her if something went wrong. It's good to be able to talk to her, and it's nice that she knows what is going on in my life. Telling her has built a lot of trust between us, and has brought us a lot closer." Catie, 17

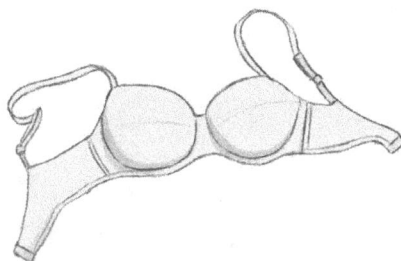

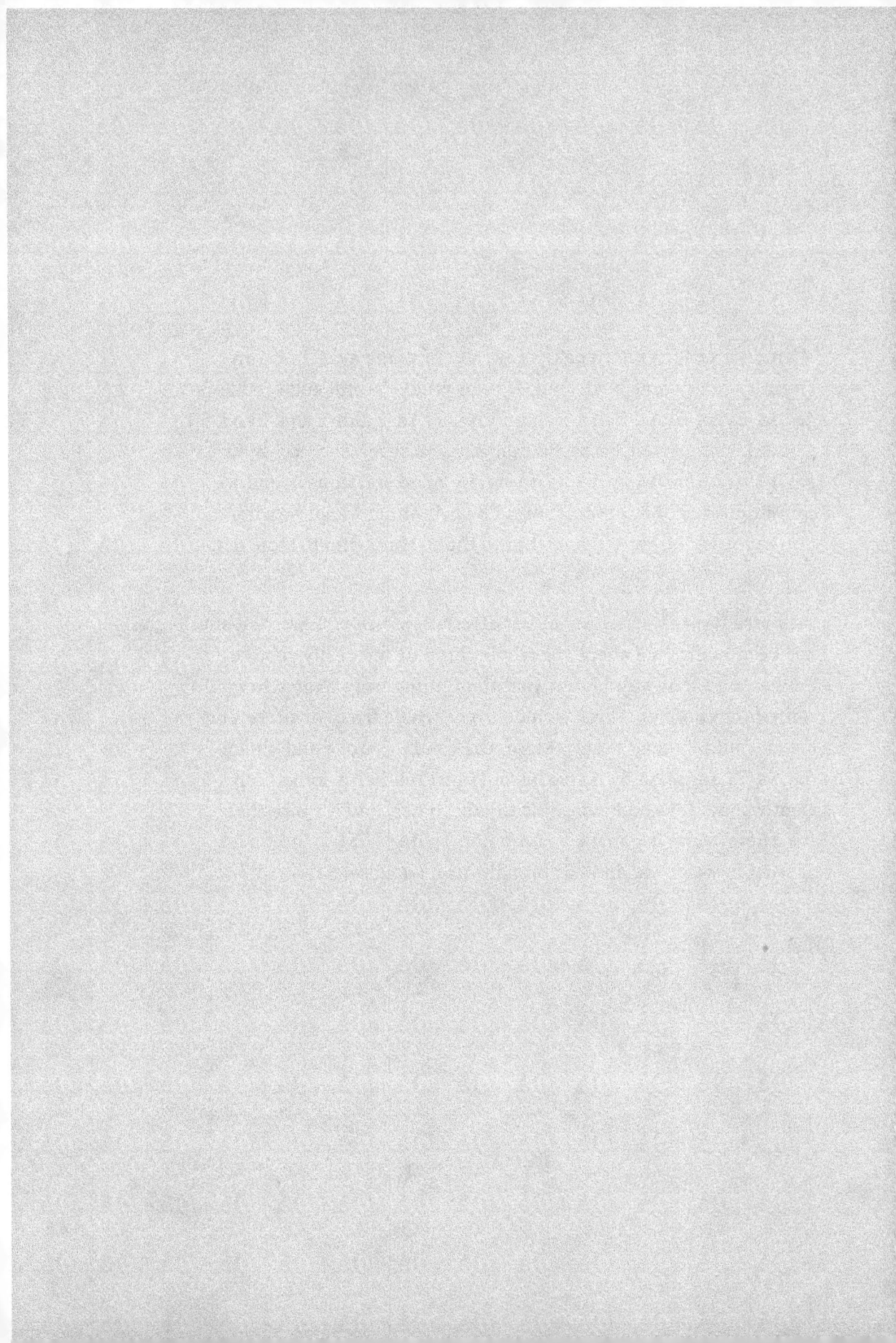

# EIGHT

# Are All the Cool Kids Really Drinking and Doing Drugs?

Just as I won't pretend you will never be interested in sex, it would be irresponsible of me to think that you won't ever be tempted to experiment with drugs and alcohol. Drug and alcohol use is really widespread, especially among teenagers. To me, one of the scariest aspects of peer pressure is the pressure to drink or take drugs, behaviors that impair our judgment, and push us to take greater risks than we would otherwise.

"I think that peer pressure can get really, really bad. Some really talented kids can lose their talents because of peer pressure. One way our society is stupid is that there are many ways that teenagers can discover drugs and alcohol. I think that the world can do without them and be much better. When people are peer pressured, they feel they have to act cool and do stuff the 'cool kids' are doing. Even if the 'cool kids' are doing something plain stupid, other kids will follow." Lizzie, 13

I won't tell you what do to or what not to do. I will only say that just as decisions about sex involve respecting your body, and making your own choices about what to do with it, decisions about drugs and alcohol involve respecting your body too. Drinking or doing drugs alters your state of mind, often lowering your inhibitions so that you do things you might otherwise not.

There are countless stories about both boys and girls who engaged in sexual activities when they were drunk or high, only to regret their actions later. The list of people who have been injured or died in drinking-related accidents is really, really long. Most of the drivers would probably not have gotten behind the wheel if they were aware of how messed up they were.

It's so easy, especially for teenagers, to think that you are not going to be affected by the risks associated with drinking or drugs. Often, teenagers tend to see themselves as invincible (unbeatable). When I was in high school, a friend of mine was in a car accident that could have been avoided if the driver had not been drinking, or if he'd been smart enough not to get behind the wheel. My friend, who was the passenger, ended up in a coma and suffered brain damage, which still affects him to this day. The driver, a close friend of his, didn't suffer nearly as much, unless you count the suffering he has endured from the guilt that he feels about what happened. I'm sure it's been tough for him. He certainly never meant to hurt anyone, but one bad decision resulted in a lot of pain and changed both of their lives. The accident was an eye-opener for all of our friends; we had known that drinking and driving were risky, but like many teenagers, we never really thought those risks would affect us.

"I have a friend who did some drugs, just one time. We talked about it, and she told me she would stop. I trusted her, and now she has started again. I'm trying to put sense into her head, but she will not listen. I've tried over and over, and I can't stop being her friend. We've been cool since pre-K. I don't know what to do. HELP!" Anonymous

The captain of my track team in high school was an amazing runner, and was offered scholarships to run at lots of great colleges. She went to visit a school that was recruiting her, and partied too hard. She got alcohol poisoning, and had to go to the hospital to have her stomach pumped. At the end of the whole ordeal she was physically fine, but she lost the scholarship offer at that school.

I'm not telling you these stories to scare you into staying away from drugs and alcohol altogether, nor do I even believe that it is realistic to think that my telling you these stories will make that happen. Exposure to drinking and drugs has become like a rite of passage for many teenagers. At some point someone will probably offer you something, and you will be faced with the decision about what to say. It's likely that you'll feel lots of peer pressure about your decision on both sides of the coin. Some of your friends will be all for trying things out, and others might judge you if you do. Either way, the most important thing is for you to think about yourself and what is best for you.

"Last summer, my friend's parents were out of town, and we were looking for something to do. We ended up at a park with some guys, and they had vodka. This was the second time I had ever had a drink, and I didn't know how alcohol could affect your body if you drink too much. I drank way too much, and started throwing up in the playground. One of the guys with us was someone who I had a bumpy past with. I felt uncomfortable around him. It was really hard to be around him, and not talk about all the stuff we needed to talk about. So every bottle that was passed to me, I just kept on drinking. It ended up being a night where I made a fool of myself in front of someone I really cared about, and wanted to talk to. I felt really sick, and someone had to walk me back to my friend's house. While I was drunk I kept thinking to myself, why did I do this? I felt helpless. I felt bad about how I couldn't handle the situation, and so I resorted to alcohol. I hate being that helpless, drunk girl. It's a disgusting feeling." Chloe, 16

I want to impress upon you that no matter how strong, smart, or capable you think you are, the risks associated with drugs and drinking apply to you too. When you make decisions about what you put in your body, you need to be fully aware of what you are doing, and value the fact that these decisions can have major consequences.

## Respect yourself

If you decide that drinking is not for you, and even if all your friends are getting wasted, know that it is okay to have made the decision you did. Don't let your friends pressure you. Be proud of your choice, and stick with it.

If you decide to try drinking or drugs, make sure that you are doing these things in a safe place. Be sure that there is a sober person around who can take care of business if something bad happens. Don't try things, especially for the first time, with a group of kids you don't know. Drinking and drugs mess with your brain, and if you are in an uncomfortable situation, you probably won't have fun anyway. Your brain will still know that you are uncomfortable, and that feeling will be part of your experience. You also need to be able to talk to people if you feel like you need help, or even just want to share what is going on for you. You won't want to do that if you don't feel safe with the people around you.

Don't mix drinking or drugs with risky activities. We've all heard a million times about the dangers of drinking and driving. This is certainly an important thing to keep in mind. But there are lots of other activities that I wouldn't advise mixing with drinking or drugs. Any activity that already has an element of risk in it: swimming, hiking on cliffs, biking—the

"No one is going to watch you the whole time and tell you not to drink too much. I am a smart girl, and I know not to drink too much. My friends know I am a smart girl, but it's up to me to make the right choices." Celia, 16

list goes on and on. Basically, I am simply trying to tell you that if you are already putting yourself at risk by drinking or doing drugs, you shouldn't be doing something that requires sharpness and attention.

## What is a drug?

A drug is a substance that, when consumed, affects your brain and alters your state of mind. Some drugs, like alcohol, nicotine, and caffeine, are legal, while others, like speed, heroin, acid (LSD), and others are illegal. Some drugs, like marijuana, psychedelic mushrooms and opium, are found in nature, while others, like cocaine, MDMA, and amphetamines, are made in labs. People take drugs for lots of different reasons. Sometimes people take them to experiment, to see how it feels to alter their state of mind. Sometimes people take drugs because they like the way the drugs make them feel. Sometimes people take drugs because they feel pressured into doing so. Sometimes people take drugs because they are addicted to them and feel they can't function normally without the drugs in their system.

Drinking or doing drugs makes you less sharp. People tend to think they can do things when they are messed up that they would never try if they were sober, like driving really fast, or running quickly through traffic. Doing these things is just plain stupid. Or people think they can handle things that they do easily when they are sober, like driving a car, or riding a bike, or even operating an oven. It might seem like you can do those things even if you are drunk, or stoned, or whatever. But it's really important to know that even if you don't feel messed up, if you took something, you probably are. It's best to chill and admit that you aren't 100 percent. Normal day-to-day activities can become risky when your mind is altered.

"I met up with my friend after school, and she had gotten a pot cookie from her friend. The cookie was green, and smelled and tasted like weed. I had about a quarter of the cookie. When it hit me, my vision blurred, and I stumbled. It felt like my brain was frozen, and like I wasn't really there. We went to another friend's house and told her that we were really high, and didn't know what to do. She gave us something to eat, and we started throwing up. I thought I was going to die, and got really sad about it. Then I accepted the fact that I was going to die. I kept throwing up, and when my parents came to pick me up I told them that I had food poisoning. Eventually I fell asleep. When I woke up I was still high, but felt okay. It was really scary, but now I am fine. I am never eating food made with pot in it again." Olivia, 16

## A word about cigarettes[1]

Nicotine—the substance found in cigarettes—is a highly addictive drug. Nicotine stimulates the heart and circulation, and has been reported to increase concentration and attention, and to decrease stress. Cigarette smoking is the greatest cause of preventable death in the United States. Tobacco users are at greater risk for lung cancer and heart disease, as well as a whole host of other problems. On average, people who smoke regularly die five to eight years earlier than people who don't. Teenagers who smoke are at increased risk of addiction (because they've started smoking so early in life), and are also twice as likely as nonsmokers to suffer from depression.

## Know your limits

Remember to remain aware of your own limits, and be sensitive to what your body can handle. Your body knows what is too much for it. If you are feeling sick, that means your body is telling you that you are hurting it or that you need to take it easy and rest. Find a place to sit or lie down, and drink some water. If you are trying something for the first time, be a minimalist! Don't take as much as other people are, just because that's what they are doing. Let your brain and body get used to the experience by just doing a little bit. Don't let people pressure you to exceed your own limits.

It's really important to keep in mind how much you've had to drink, or how much of a drug you've taken. It's easy to lose track as your brain becomes less connected to reality, and this can lead to trouble. Stay aware of what you are putting in your body, and stop when you feel you've had enough. I knew someone in college who used to keep all the bottle caps from the beers he drank that night in his pocket. That way, if he lost track, he could just look in his pocket. It's a pretty good idea: you can know what you've had without having to worry about remembering. If you do too much, the experience will no longer be fun. You'll just be sick.

**Know what you are taking**

Because most drugs are illegal, it's difficult to know what you are getting. If you decide to try drugs, do so wisely. Don't take something from someone you don't know, and always ask exactly what it is that you are getting. There are places that will test various drugs to make sure they are safe and legitimate. This is a really good idea.

Even when drinking, you need to be serious about knowing what you are getting. If you are in a crowded party or an unfamiliar situation, don't leave your drink behind and go back for it later. You never know what might have been dropped in there. Don't take drinks from someone you don't know. I may seem paranoid, I know, but there are tons of stories of girls whose drinks were spiked with all sorts of drugs, and then the girls got taken advantage of when they were really messed up.

"I've seen lots of people get really sick from drinking. When I drink, I pay close attention to how much I am having. I can't say I know my limit, but I stop before I ever reach it." Olivia, 16

### Be honest

If you are going to drink or do drugs, tell the friends you are with what you are doing, even if you think they are going to judge you. That way, if something happens, they will have the information they may need later if you need some support. Even if you think you might get in trouble, it's worth it to be truthful about what is in your body so that you can get the help you need.

If you are in trouble, don't hesitate to call someone who can help you, like your parents. Even if they get angry with you later, it's worth it to have your parents pick you up if you or your driver is too drunk to get behind the wheel. The last thing your parents want is to see you hurt—or worse, dead—so chances are they will try to help you out, even if they are upset with you.

"I don't think that smoking pot is necessarily bad, and I admit that I enjoy the effects I feel from smoking pot. But I have limits about how much I will smoke, and how often. I only smoke when I am with certain friends. At the same time, I know that smoking has effects on learning, and recognize that it makes me feel stupid the next day. I also don't like when people smoke because they have nothing to do." Carrie, 16

## Stay away from sex

Drinking and/or doing drugs changes the way we think about
things, and tends to lower our inhibitions. It's really easy to
forget our own limits—especially in terms of sex—and get
carried away. This might mean forgetting what we want for
ourselves, and doing things we wouldn't do if we were sober.
Or it might mean being less strong about saying no to someone
if we are being pressured. Either way, it is all too easy to end
up in a bad situation. My advice to you is to avoid engaging in
sexual activities when your mind isn't 100 percent.

"I have a friend who lost her virginity when she was drunk, and I
feel bad for her. She came back to my house afterward, and I felt
really good that I could be there for her. I knew that if I was in
that situation, it would help to have a friend there to assure me
that people make those kinds of mistakes all the time." Connie, 16

## Be aware

Adolescence can be a very stressful time, and one of the easiest
ways to avoid dealing with stress is to pretend it doesn't exist.
There is a big difference between trying something a few times
and doing it all the time. Getting high on drugs every day or
being drunk all the time can help you hide from your problems,
and might make the world seem easier to handle. But it is

definitely not a healthy solution. If you think you are doing something too much, or if you think one of your friends is in trouble, talk to someone you trust. You can get help, both with your drinking/drug problem as well as with the stress that might be causing the problem. The most important thing to keep in mind is that you are not alone; many other people have suffered like you. Help is out there. You just have to be willing to accept it. A good place to start is the hotline for Phoenix House (www.phoenixhouse.org), a national, nonprofit provider of substance abuse services. Their number is 1-888-671-9392.

\*\*\*

Most importantly, **always respect yourself**. You know how to make good decisions about your own life as long as you listen to your inner voice. Listen to yourself and do what feels right to you; the best decision comes from your heart.

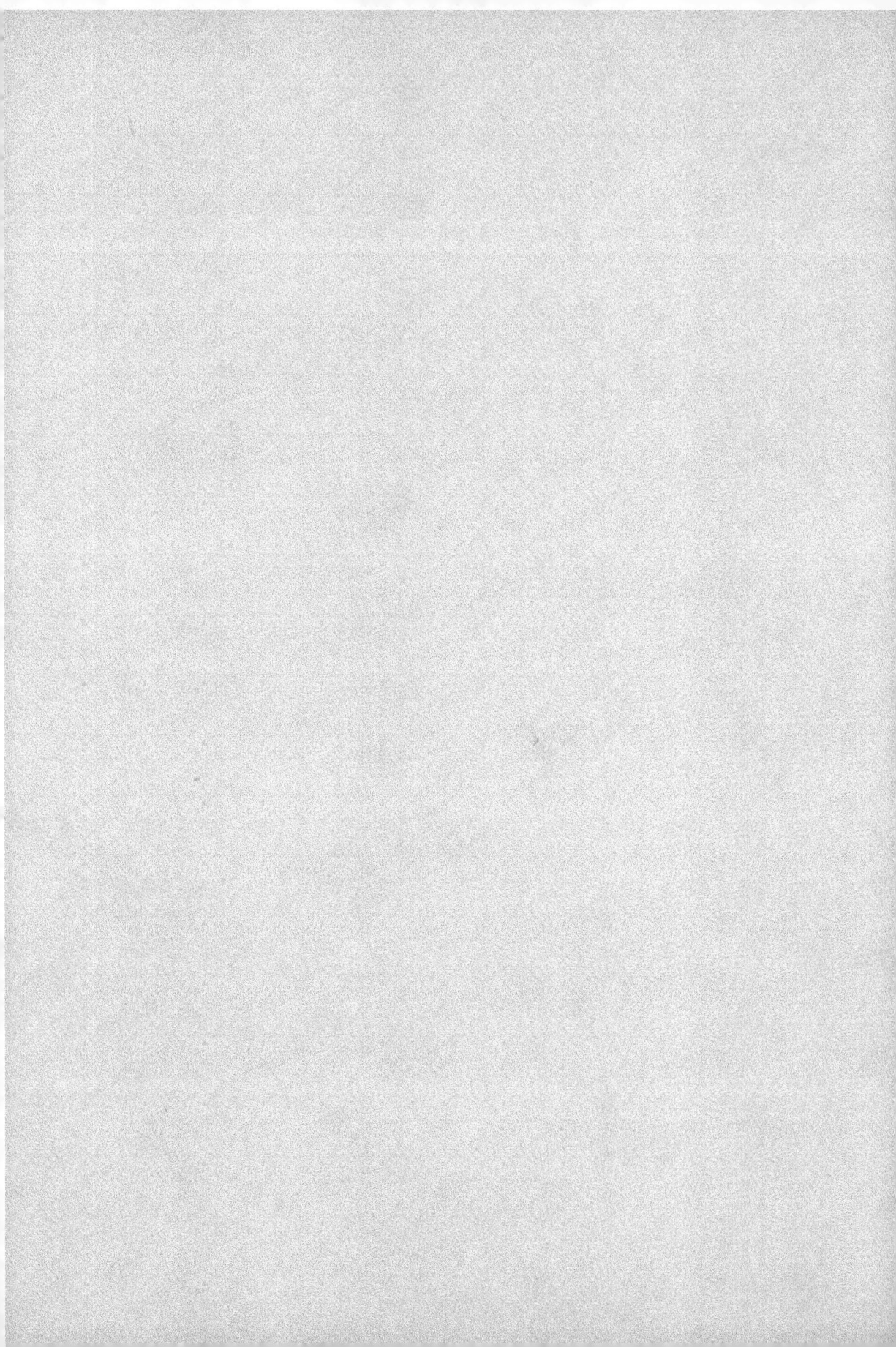

NINE

# I'm so STRESSED!

The stresses we feel as adolescents can have a major impact on us. We experience a ton of different pressures, and it is easy to feel overwhelmed. Our peers, our parents, our teachers, and our society all have ideas about how we should live and behave. We absorb all of these pressures, and then try our best to make decisions for ourselves about what we want. It's difficult—if not impossible—to figure out what is best for us when there are so many influences telling us how to be and what to do.

"I get stressed when it feels like everything is happening all at once. I also get stressed when my friends are mad at me, because then I might not have anyone to talk to when I am upset." Maia, 13

"What stresses me out? People killing themselves to look 'perfect.' People killing themselves to be popular. Homework. Home is for fun and school is for work. Teachers, getting you in trouble for the smallest things." Liana, 13

"When I have to pack up to go to my mom's or dad's house, I get stressed. I have to bring half my clothes, my school stuff, my soccer stuff, and just other stuff I need. It's stressful because forgetting things I need at one house is really annoying, and I have to start a completely different week with one of my parents. I also get stressed out when I am in a fight with my friends because I get worried about the next day." Emma, 13

"Dance class stresses me out. People asking me to do things I don't want to do. Wanting to be a good friend to people. Trying to look pretty all the time. School and homework stress me out. Taking care of my brother and sister. Doing things my close friends want me to." Samantha, 13

"Things that stress me out are not getting enough sleep, because then I can't concentrate on anything. Trying to make people like me stresses me out." Eliza, 13

"Stress is when you don't know what to do. It's a mental brain block that leaves you hanging. Confused. Stress is when you cry over simple homework. Stress is when you hate everything you look at. Stress is not being able to sleep at night. Stress is when you want to scream all the time. Stress takes you over. It's the side of you that can't or won't let you succeed. Waiting for you to mess up or get angry with your best friends. Stress is when you don't know what to do because EVERYTHING seems to go wrong." Benazir, 13

Whoa! I'm stressed just from writing all that stuff down. It's pretty unbelievable how much pressure adolescents experience. Not that adults don't experience stress—we do. But a huge difference between adults and adolescents, especially in terms of stress, is that adults are more often able to put things in perspective, to see things for what they really are.

I mean, there are a million things that are causing stress in my life right now, but I can look at them, and know that they'll work out. I can put things in perspective, and understand that even though I am overwhelmed right now, there will be a time when things will be calmer. (In fact, as I edit this chapter, a few months after I first wrote it, I can safely say that most of the things that were stressing me out when I originally wrote it have been resolved.) As an adolescent, I could only see the moment. I only knew what was hurting me right at that second, and couldn't imagine that at some point in the future, things would work out for the best.

## Friend stress

I can especially relate to feeling stressed about fighting with my friends. I remember spending many nights tossing and turning in my bed, unsure as to whether my friends would talk to me the next day. It was the worst feeling, not knowing what the morning would bring. I mean, what was the deal? Why couldn't my friends just be my friends?

I remember feeling that there was nothing more important than being popular. As I described in earlier chapters, I stayed friends with kids who treated me like trash because being in their clique meant being popular. I am not even sure why being popular was so important. All it really meant for me was that I had to act like I was too cool to hang out with a lot of other kids whom I actually liked. It also meant that I had to wear whatever we decided we'd wear on specific days. Looking back, I realize that the whole thing was pretty ridiculous, but it seemed really important at the time.

But I've spent enough time in this book talking about friends and meanness and cliques. I just want to remind you to try as hard as you can to stay true to yourself, and know that, no matter what anyone else thinks, you are a person who deserves to be loved, and treated with respect. People who aren't giving you love and respect don't deserve your time or energy. If you want to read more about this, check back in Chapter Four and Chapter Five.

## School stress

And then there's school. Why are the teachers so annoying? Who will I sit with at lunch? Why is there so much homework? Why do I feel like I have to be the best at everything all the time? What do I do when I am not the best?

First of all, let me remind you that I'm a teacher, and believe with all of my heart that education is one of the most important aspects of any society. However, I also think that the way schools evaluate students, by assigning grades, creates a stressful situation for most kids and families. I mean, think about it: we ask kids to learn because we believe that what we are teaching them is valuable, and will help them in their lives. We want to help students to develop a particular set of skills, or acquire certain information. It is easier for some kids to learn those skills than others, but we judge them all in the same way.

I try not to give grades, and when I have to, I try to base the grades that I give on effort, because I recognize that some students learn more quickly than others. In many schools, though, teachers look at students who are failing and penalize them with bad grades rather than supporting them with extra help and more resources. This is definitely not true across the board, and many schools are making efforts to be more supportive and less judgmental. But the current system of grading is, without a doubt, a major cause of stress.

Grades create another reason to compete. As if that's what we need in our world today! I could write a whole other book about grades. But for the time being, I think it is enough to say that, as a teacher, I recognize the problems grades cause. What's more is that, in many places, there is increased competition in school, not just about grades, but also about getting into the next level of school, be it high school or college. Application processes in which you have to basically sum up your entire being on paper for someone to judge, and decide whether you are worthy of attending their school, are guaranteed stress builders. The most important thing I can say is to try your best to take the whole thing in stride and always remember that evaluations rarely reflect how much you really know.

Stress is a state of mind that results from your reactions to situations, not from the situations themselves. If you can keep that in your head, I think it will be a lot easier to remain calm about things that are related to school.

"Ask anyone in my class, I am the most stressed out person ever. When I am stressed or angry, I pretty much do everything but explode. I hate it when I am having massive computer problems right before something is due. Art class is pretty much the worst class ever, because I can't do anything. The teacher is always helping all the kids who are way ahead, rather than kids who are way behind. And then she completely ignores everything I am trying to tell her.

"I hate when nothing seems to be going right. I hate it when I
have to do my homework on Sunday night because Saturdays
aren't good for homework, and I go with my dad on Sundays, and
he doesn't want me to do homework. Stress really does suck."
Medina, 13

## A few things to keep in mind

> Learn for the sake of learning. Do what interests you, both in school
and after school. Try your best and be diligent about your work.

> Know that learning how to study is really important, and will help you
in many aspects of life that extend far beyond school. Doing work that
may seem pointless or annoying can be helpful, because it forces you to
explore a subject that may not have seemed interesting at first. You will
need this skill in the future, more than you can imagine.

> If you challenge yourself to try things that are difficult, you will
succeed, even in areas you never thought possible.

> Take pride in the work you do, and try to take grades for what they
usually are: numbers and letters that are often little indication of how
much you really understand.

> Try to play the game as best you can. Do what you need to do in order
to succeed, and try not to let all the competition get under your skin.

"Best friends, friends, and enemies stress me out. I feel like I'm in a tug-of-war. One minute I am pulling them toward me. They refuse. The next minute, I'm pushing them away, while they try to pull me back. Enemies are always throwing insults at each other, glaring, and giving the silent treatment." Alexis, 13

### Parent stress

Let's not forget our parents! Now, don't get me wrong. I love my parents. They are wonderful people. They care about me very much, and I owe them my life. That said, there was little that caused me more stress in my adolescence than my relationship with my parents. Our interactions were often negative. I was constantly frustrated by the way we dealt with each other, because I felt that no matter how hard I tried to get them to listen to me, they never really heard what I was saying. Even though I knew they loved me, I also felt that they had no clue what was going on in my head, that they didn't get me. I could not figure out how to explain my thoughts or feelings to them in a way that they would understand. In part, this feeling was about me not getting what I wanted all the time. It's easy to think that your parents aren't listening to you if they don't see why you need to spend as much time as possible with your friends, for example. In retrospect, I recognize that I should not have been allowed to do whatever I wanted all the time, and I do see that my parents had a point when they set limits for me. At the time, though, I thought that my parents didn't care about me.

I don't want to make any unfair assumptions about what your situation with your parents is like. But I do want to tell you about my own experiences. Maybe that will give you some insight into what is going on in your family. When I was an adolescent, I didn't really allow my parents to support me as much as I probably should have. I distanced myself from them, instead of reaching out for help. My dad had never been an adolescent girl, and didn't understand the stresses I was experiencing. He had no way to see the world through my eyes. Though my mom had, of course, been an adolescent girl, we weren't getting along well at the time. I spent much more energy fighting with her than being close with her.

So, during middle school and much of high school, I fought with my parents fairly regularly, and found myself yelling and screaming at them more than I found myself speaking with them calmly. I was annoyed or embarrassed by everything they did. I think many adolescent girls have similar experiences. We often feel like we are at war with our parents—especially our moms—and try as hard as we can to keep them out of our personal lives.

During adolescence, the people who look after us, especially our parents, can seem like the biggest pain ever because we want to assert our independence and lead our own lives, while they want to take care of us. I wanted to be in total control of my time, and was not at all happy about my parents telling me what to do. At the same time, we are still kids. We don't have jobs that pay the bills, we live in our parents' houses, and we aren't fully capable of taking care of ourselves. I know you are reading this and thinking, "Of course I can take care of myself!" But in all seriousness, do you have any idea how you might get health insurance if you were to leave your parents' care? Or get a job that would cover your expenses if you haven't yet earned a high school diploma? And anyway, I think most of us would rather have our parents and guardians there for us, even if there are a whole lot of emotions swirling around.

So as adolescents we find ourselves stuck between being kids and being adults. And it's hard to know how to fit our parents into that mix. It's natural to resist them, and feel anger toward them for telling us what to do. It's normal to feel that they don't understand us, because in many ways, they don't. They aren't where we are, inside our heads. We don't really help the situation either, because—at least in my case—I barely tried to talk calmly with my parents during adolescence. I did way more yelling than I should have, and often assumed that they wouldn't listen to me if I didn't yell.

The point I am trying to make is that, while I definitely do not have all the answers, it is important to recognize a few things. First and foremost, our parents, for the most part, want what is best for us, and really do love us, even if they don't always give us what we ask for. Furthermore, I know, at least in my own situation, that I contributed a great deal to the stress in my relationship with my family. I was completely unwilling to recognize that at the time. I was sure that everything was their fault.

Remember that your parents are your allies, and should be on your side, even when you are completely horrible to them. They are parents; that's their job. As their child, it's your job to try to love your parents, and know that they are there for you. Tolerate the little things that annoy you about them, and trust them to take care of you. After all, they've gotten you this far, right?

At the same time, some people have really difficult relationships with their parents, and those relationships can be a great source of stress. Other people don't have relationships with their parents for a wide variety of reasons. Try to find an adult that you can talk to so you can get the support you need. When we are adolescents, we may think we don't need adults in our lives, but we do. If your parents really aren't able to give you the love and support you need, talk to someone else in your

> "My parents are too strict. My parents don't listen to me."
> **Liza, 13**

family, or to a teacher or counselor. Recognize that you will greatly benefit from the support of a caring adult, even if he or she is not your parent.

I was too foolish to let my mom help me as much as she could have during my adolescence, but my sister was much calmer, and benefited a great deal from my mother's wisdom. If you can't let them in, that's okay too. But try not to be too harsh about pushing them out. Feeding a bad relationship only causes more stress in your life—something you definitely don't need. If you're not getting along with your parents, just try to stay calm. Try to do your own thing: spend time on your own and do things that make you happy; try to take your mind off of your stress.

**Some ideas about what to do when you are really angry with your parents**

> Take a deep breath.

> Imagine yourself somewhere beautiful that makes you happy.

> Go for a walk.

> Take a moment (or a few hours) to have some space from your parents; even if you can't leave, just try to block them out, and be alone in your mind.

> Write in your journal.

> Call a friend.

> Cry and let your emotions out.

> Talk to your brother or sister.

## Important things to look for

Stress has a more serious effect on some people than it does on others. It is really important to keep an eye out to make sure you (and your friends) are healthy, and that life isn't taking too harsh a toll on you.

Certainly, life can seem hard at times, and can get you down, especially if you are a person who is easily overwhelmed. This is normal. But if you find yourself feeling really down more often than not, you might be experiencing depression. Depression is a clinical term for a psychological disorder characterized by an ongoing feeling of being upset—in other words, almost always feeling sad. In some cases, depression is a minor problem and can pass on its own. Sometimes, though, depression can get really serious, and you might need to get help to deal with it.

## Some things that could put you at risk for depression[1]

> A family history of depression

> Losing a parent, or someone else close to you

> The breakup of a romantic relationship

> Being injured, or dealing with chronic illness

> Experiencing abuse or neglect

> Fighting in your family

> Dealing with lots of stress

> Parents getting divorced

> Smoking cigarettes, abusing drugs or alcohol

> Wondering about your sexual identity

> A traumatic event, such as a car accident, a robbery, or a rape

### What can you do about it?

**Talk to an adult you trust**. Tell a teacher, counselor, friend, parent, priest, rabbi or whomever you choose, how you are feeling. I know this might seem scary, but talking about what you are going through is the first step to feeling better.

\*\*\*

**Get professional help**. Find a counselor, therapist, or doctor. Again, the first step to getting this help is talking to an adult you trust. S/he can help you find a professional with whom you can talk.

**Stay connected to friends and family.** Even though you might want to be alone a lot, friends and family can help you to keep it together, and remind you of your good qualities, even if it is hard for you to see them yourself.

***

**Accept that depression is not your fault**. Depression is a medical condition, which doesn't come from a lack of willpower or a personal flaw.

***

**Take care of yourself**. Make sure that you are sleeping at least eight hours a night, and eating well-balanced meals every day. Even if you don't feel hungry, eating—at least a little—will help you to stay healthy. Make an effort to get some exercise, even if you don't feel like it. Exercising releases hormones in your body that make you feel better.

***

**Express your feelings**. Talk to a friend or write in a journal or draw or dance or sing—whatever is most comfortable for you. Plan to do something fun, so you have something to look forward to every day.

## How do I know if I'm depressed?[2]

> Have you been feeling sad, anxious, or empty inside?

> Have you been losing interest in things that were once fun and exciting?

> Have you been feeling increasingly angry?

> Have you been having trouble getting along with your family and friends?

> Has your appetite changed, causing you to gain or lose weight?

> Has your energy level changed, causing you to be really tired, restless, or irritable?

> Have your sleep patterns changed, either sleeping a lot more or a lot less?

> Do you find yourself getting up really early in the morning, unable to go back to sleep?

> Have you been feeling really bad about yourself, or been really hard on yourself lately?

> Have you been thinking a lot about death and dying?

If you've been feeling any of these ways for two weeks or longer, know that help is available. Depression can be treated with therapy (talking to a psychologist or counselor), medication, or a combination of both. With the right treatment, the majority of people who reach out for help get better. Depression is not something you have to deal with forever. You can change your state of mind and reconnect with the positive energy to enjoy your life.

## Alcohol and drugs

If you're depressed, you might have a problem with alcohol and/or drugs. Sometimes depression comes first, and drugs are an attempt to feel better, or hide from your problems. Other times, drinking or doing drugs comes first. Regardless of which comes first, if you're drinking alcohol or using drugs, and think you may be depressed, it is important to admit to yourself that you may have a problem, and that it's time to deal with it. Even if drinking or doing drugs makes you feel better in the short term, it is only a temporary solution, and may actually hurt you in the long term.

## Suicide

Thoughts of death or suicide can be signs of depression. If you are depressed, it's normal to think about suicide and death, but that doesn't mean that you shouldn't get help. If you feel like you can't cope anymore, or that life isn't worth living, it's important to find someone to help you out. Contact someone you trust, such as a friend, parent or other relative, teacher, coach, advisor, or anyone else you feel comfortable talking with. You can also call a suicide hotline. There are lots of local numbers you can find on the Internet or in your phone book, or you can try the National Suicide Hotline's USA phone number: 1-800-273-TALK (1-800-273-8255). If you think you or someone you know is in immediate danger, call 911, or go to an emergency room.

**Hurting yourself**

Lots of people who are depressed take their sadness about life out on themselves by hurting themselves. There are a number of common ways that people do this, including obsessively pulling out their hair, carving words or pictures into their bodies, or cutting themselves compulsively.

Almost every time I have worked with a group of young women, I have had a student who has cut herself. Cutting (and all other ways of hurting yourself) is no joke, and needs to be taken seriously. It's important enough to say it again: cutting yourself is no joke, and needs to be taken seriously. Doing harm to yourself is a red flag that you need help. It's way too easy to be embarrassed, and try to hide your problems from people you trust and love, and even from yourself. When you get into a mental state that is unhealthy, it's easy to blame yourself, and feel like a freak for thinking the things you do. I've been there, and I know how hard it is to feel okay about feeling bad. But recognizing that you have a problem is the first step to finding a solution. What's the next step? Talk to someone you trust.

## One girl's story

One student of mine, whose name I won't share for the sake of her privacy, came to me after class one day to talk. We had read a story about a girl who was bulimic, and had also cut herself. The girl in the story was dealing with some pretty heavy stuff, and was blaming herself, even though her problems were not her fault. She cut herself to punish herself for being bulimic.

My student hung around after class to talk to me about the story, and then began to share her own story with me. She told me that the year before, her brother had been murdered as a result of gang violence. After her brother died, she said, a part of her mom died too. Her mom didn't love life like she used to, and was sad all the time. My student felt like she had to keep her own sadness inside, because she didn't want to upset her mom. In an effort to deal with all this, she cut herself, not too severely, but enough to make herself bleed.

She was telling me this story a year after she'd cut herself, and said she had never done it again. Luckily, she didn't hurt herself too badly physically, but she was definitely carrying around some serious emotional baggage. She told me that I was the first person who she'd talked to about cutting herself, and about how

she was feeling in general. She cried the whole time we talked, but at the end of our conversation, she said she felt better. I encouraged her to talk to her parents, which she did that night.

Together with the principal of her school, I found her a professional to talk to, and also found some help for her family. I know that it was really hard for her to be honest with me, and especially to tell me that she'd cut herself. She was embarrassed about what she'd done. I am very proud of her for coming to me, and I know that she is doing much better now. I think she would say that although it was tough to open up about things she had been keeping inside for a whole year, she is glad that she did.

I know that the hardest part of this is taking that very first step—actually telling someone what is going on with you. It can be embarrassing and stressful to think about sharing your darkest secrets with someone else. It took my student an entire year to do it, but in the end, I think she'd agree that it was much worse to suffer with her secret alone than to get help. The first step is definitely the hardest. But once you do it, you will feel much better. No one can help you unless you let them know that you need them.

## Getting and staying happy

All in all, we need to count our blessings. Keep an eye on what is good in our lives, and be thankful for those positive things. Keep it all in perspective; no matter how bad things seem, they will get better. There will be a time when all the stresses and headaches will pass, and you will not feel so bent out of shape. The circumstances may not even need to change, but the way that you react to them can make a world of difference. I've been through a lot in my life, but I still believe that no time was more challenging than adolescence. I felt like I was alone in the world. To me, there is no worse feeling than that. Luckily, that time has passed. Life has gotten better. There are still rough spots, but I now have ways to deal with them. Until all this passes—and it will—know that there are ways to find happiness in the midst of all the madness.

**Taking care of yourself**

> Do things that make you happy.

> Take time for yourself.

> Go outside and hang out in a park or at the beach.

> Spend time with a close friend.

> Read a book.

> Dance.

> Laugh.

> Most importantly, smile as much as possible. You will automatically feel better.

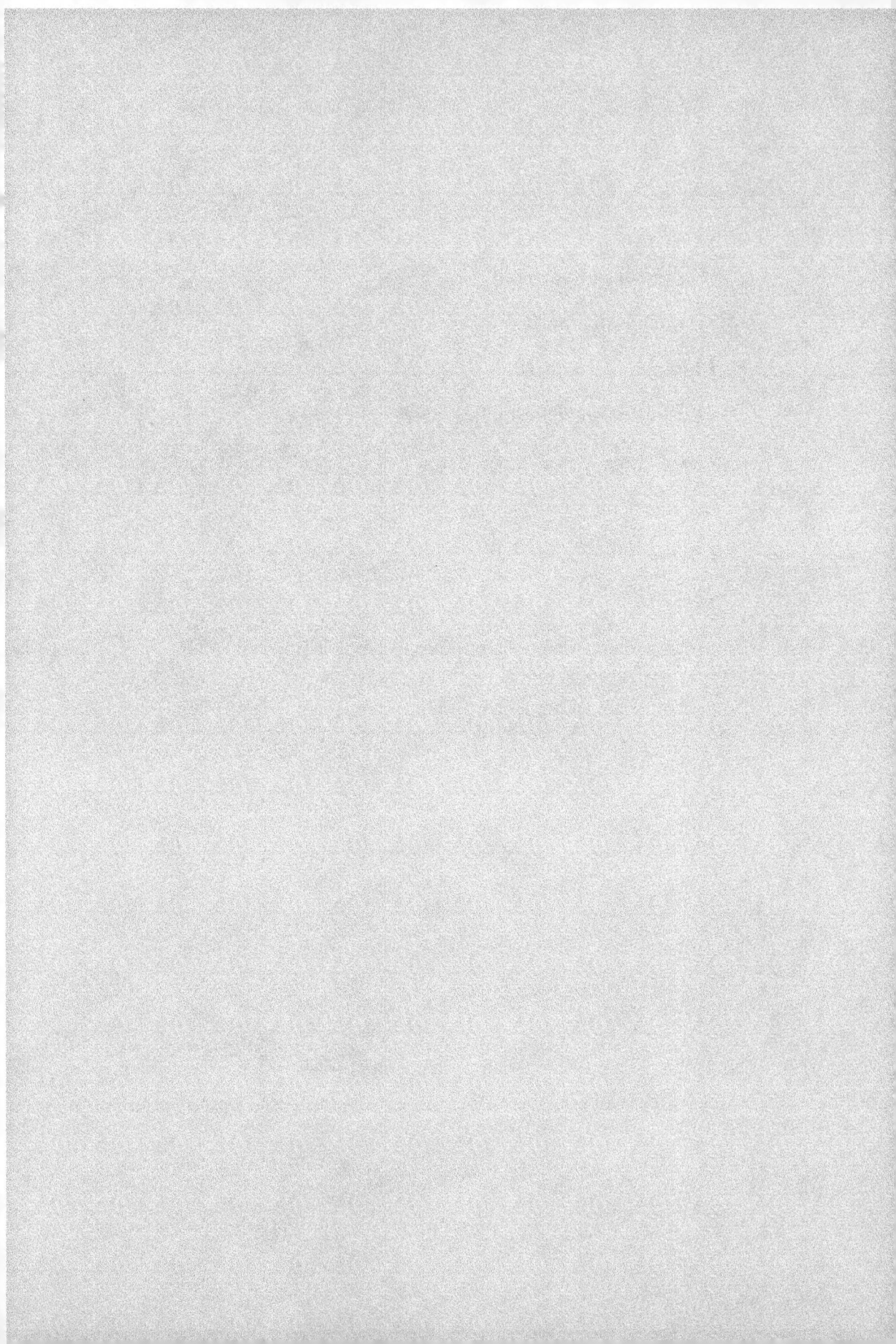

TEN

# How Does My Identity
# Influence Me?

In my life, I have met many people who have taught me many things. In fact, it seems contradictory for a teacher to say this, but most of what I've learned over the course of my life on this planet has been from my relationships with others, rather than from school. I have gained immeasurable understanding from my students, parents, teachers, friends, and enemies.

There are always some relationships that stand out, that change how you see things. When I went to college, I was nineteen, and for the first time in my life, I entered a world in which I was not a member of the majority. I had lived my whole life close to New York City, in a town where Jews are in the majority, and had then spent a year after high school studying and volunteering in Israel. Even though I went to a public high school, the town I lived in was mostly Jewish, and I never had to defend my identity or explain my background to my friends, even those who were not Jewish.

While I was in college, I developed friendships with people who were different from the people I knew from home. As my friendships deepened, I learned to see myself with new eyes. While my friends from home were somewhat diverse, we were products of a similar education and most of us came from similar backgrounds. My new friendships helped me learn about different ways of life and different perspectives—and encouraged me to question my own.

For me, one of the most significant reflections of my time in college was about what it means to be white in America, and how different that is from being a person of color. The closer I became with a few specific friends of color, the more I recognized the hidden racism in my community.

People who grew up in my hometown tend to have racist attitudes because they grew up seeing the world through a certain set of eyes, eyes that are used to privilege and opportunity, eyes that see people of color as excluded from many opportunities. It would have been rare to hear a racial slur in the halls of my high school, but it would have also been pretty rare to see black kids and white kids hanging out together as close friends. We lived in a world that had an underground racism, one that people didn't really talk about, but that we all knew existed.

When my friend Victor (who is black) got into a good college, other kids automatically discredited his success, quietly whispering behind his back that he got in "because he's black." Never mind the fact that Victor is really smart and capable, and did very well in school.

When a friend who is black came to my house one year for Thanksgiving, I felt compelled to explain to her that if we drove around the neighborhood together, most people would automatically assume that she was my housekeeper. It hurt me to tell her this, but it hurt me even more to hear that she already knew. For me, race was an issue to discuss, an abstract subject to think about. For my friends of color, race is not something to think about as detached from one's life—it is an inherent part of their lived experience.

I know that being an adolescent girl in this country is different if you are not white, especially when the standard of beauty the media transmits to us is so clearly white. Women of color are portrayed exotically in the media. I know how this makes me feel, and I know how it has made many of my students feel, including students of color. But I don't live their experience.

To be completely honest, as a white woman, I don't think that I am qualified to write this chapter. But I didn't want to leave out the issue of race. I think that being a woman of color presents unique challenges, imposed by our societal expectations and reinforced by stereotypes. I think that women of color are judged by a standard of beauty that is even more unrealistic than the standard by which white women are judged. But, again, what I have to say about race comes from my perceptions, not my experience—what I've seen, not what I've lived.

"A white girl that has money, a black girl with no daddy and great basketball skills. What am I? I'm a Latina, not black or white but brown. Latina means you have to be enough American for the Americans, enough Latin for your roots, and you have to be ghetto enough to live in the streets. It means eating beans and rice three nights a week. It means having a quinceañera, and months later you're pregnant. It means living in a house that has the smell of tortillas and warm Mexican bread. It means each Sunday you have a nice dress to wear, and you have two long beautiful Aztec braids that reach your back. It means your dad tells you you're beautiful, and that you don't need makeup to make you look beautiful. It means you sneak makeup behind your mama's back, and put it on at school. It means you have to be down for one gang color. It means you have to dance as good as black girls. It means you have the way you talk when you are around the ghetto girls around the hood. It means you have to know how to cook at the age of ten years old. It means you have to get married to the old gentleman that your mom knew ever since he was small.

"It means you cannot go out with a black guy. It means you have to have a big family after you get married. It means doing ALL the chores around the house. It means you have to know how to dance to Latin music. It means you have to teach English to all the Latinos in your country. It means you get to go to college because of a major turnaround that you did, and received a scholarship." Sayra, 15

The society in which we live is influenced by all of the people who live in it, whose traditions and identities help inform our shared culture. Yet, sometimes, we learn to be afraid of what is different and reject the other. For white people, who make up the dominant group, the topic of race is often considered taboo. We don't talk about the cultural norms that keep racism alive. For those of us in the dominant group, it is our responsibility to understand that we can perpetuate these norms OR help to disrupt the status quo by engaging in conscious conversations that help us identify our own biases and prejudices. Our shared journey is to try to find the common ground between us, to see that we are all humans, and to live together in that understanding.

When we judge someone else because of the color of her skin, the way she dresses, the accent with which she speaks—we create an obstacle that prevents us from really meeting the other. We see others through the lens of our opinions and prejudices, instead of seeing them for who they really are. True connection between people is possible only through acceptance. Judgement creates isolation and perpetuates hatred. That's not the legacy I hope to leave for future generations.

"Growing up as a young black female, I realized at an early age that
death lived around the corner, and pain right next door. Death
was dodge-able for me but polluted my personal world, which
consisted of a few friends and family members. As for pain, it was
irresistible, spreading within my soul like a disease. Being a young
black female, I was told I wasn't enough of a woman because of my
naturalness. I was told that the untamable mane I was born with
had to be straight, and that I had to maintain my weight under
125 pounds. I was told that I had to have long, flowing hair, and
be completely hairless everywhere besides my head. I was told that
black was not acceptable, let alone beautiful. Soon enough I was
molded into conformity with popular culture—I only weigh 107
pounds, and I'm completely hairless in places other than my head.
I hope they're happy! They have taken over my innocent image,
but I refuse to let them take over my mind!

"Believe it or not, many young black women are brainwashed by
the media. We are told that we are not beautiful enough, yet we
are beautiful enough to pose around in a thong and bounce that
ass. We are also told that we are not smart enough, but we are used
for our brilliant ideas. Nevertheless, we understand that beauty
is in the eye of the beholder, and that no matter what they say or
do, they cannot and will not possess our minds. We know that we
are brilliant beings, which the world needs. We beautiful young
black females understand that compromise is necessary, and that

our natural appearance is secretly worshipped. As a result, we have decided that we'll put up a facade for a little while, because the world isn't ready yet. When we reveal our natural and ultimate beauty, the world will have to squint lest it will be blinded." Rena, 15

Again, I speak humbly, because I am only talking about what I've observed as a white woman. But I've certainly seen that for my students of color, the issues that affect any teenager are further complicated by the racist and sexist attitudes in our society. Some of those attitudes are obvious, and others are hidden, like when a store clerk quietly watches people of color to make sure they aren't stealing, or another customer assumes that they work there, rather than shop there, just because they are not white. However, from Rena, Sayra, and many other young women of color, I have learned that despite the struggles, it is possible to find the sense of self-confidence we all need to carry ourselves gracefully in this world.

When we see difference, we can choose to see the beauty that exists in a diverse world, a world comprised of people who come from different places and have different perspectives. We don't always need to agree, but we do need to respect. This respect honors difference. When we honor difference, we can celebrate it and enjoy the gifts we receive from our own culture, share them with others and learn from the gifts they share with us. This exchange enriches our lives.

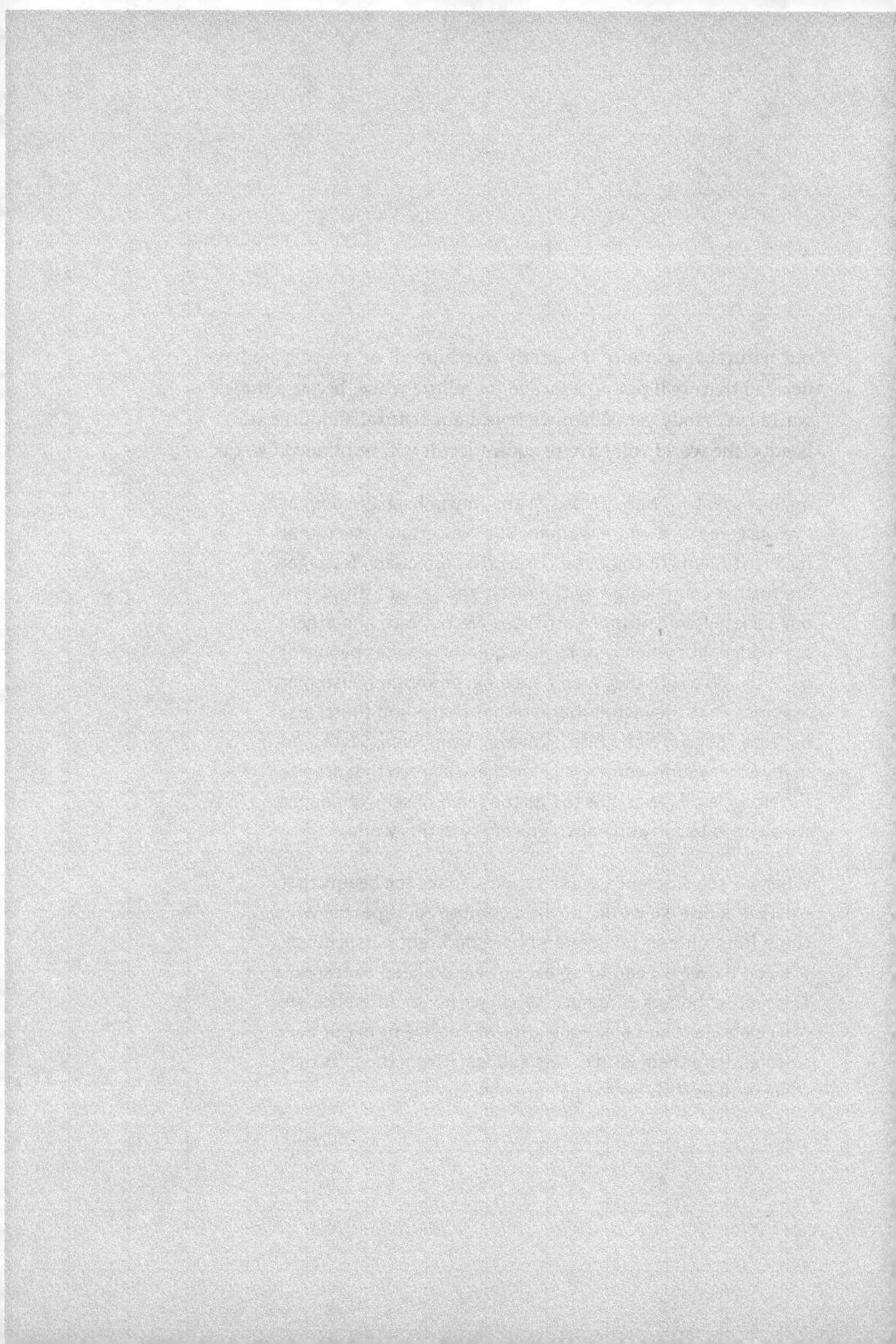

# ELEVEN

# Family, Friends
# and that Significant Other

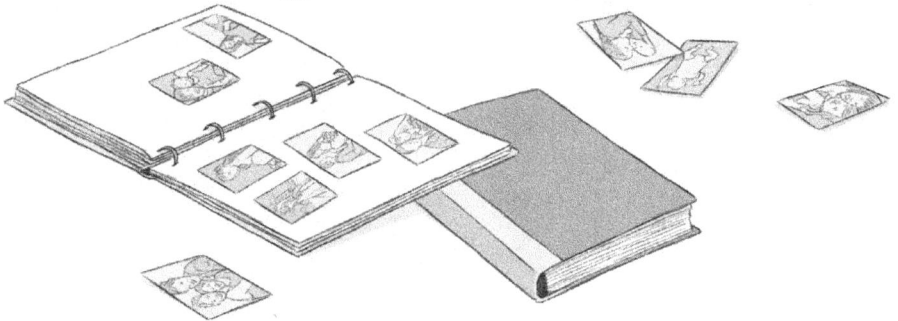

There are millions of groupings of people that define themselves as families. Some families have two parents, some have one. Sometimes the two parents are both moms, sometimes they are both dads. Sometimes they are married, sometimes they are not. Sometimes two-parent families split up, and become two one-parent families. Sometimes those one-parent families grow to include a second parent, and sometimes a few extra kids. Some families have lots of kids, some have only one. In some families, children are adopted; in others, everyone is biologically related.

No matter who makes up your family, the thing that makes it a family is that its members have unique and intense relationships with one another. Every family is different, and there is no standard that defines how people in families should act. The relationships among family members are often a big mix of intense feelings.

I am lucky to have a family that has supported me throughout all of the different stages of my life. Certainly, my parents and sister have their opinions about the choices I make, and they don't usually hesitate to express those opinions. Sometimes I listen to them, and sometimes I don't, but my reactions to their feelings are always a complicated combination of emotions. I never want to hurt my parents or sister, but sometimes I don't agree with them.

## Parents

Throughout our lives, relationships with our parents are complicated. I am not a parent, and can't pretend to know how it feels to be one. I can only imagine that it is quite intense. Think about it from their side: here is this child they created, or adopted, and raised. Of course, they want the best for the child, and work really hard to provide that. Imagine how it must feel when the child doesn't want what the parent thinks is best. On one hand, parents should be glad they've raised children who can make their own decisions. On the other, I'm sure they can't help but worry all the time about whether their children will make the right decisions. Being a parent is really difficult and complicated. We need to remember that, and cut our parents some slack when they are not perfect. No one is. It's not fair for us to expect them to be.

When I was an adolescent, I felt constantly torn between wanting to do my own thing and wanting my parents to be proud of me. A big part of being an adolescent is about forging your own path, figuring out who you are, and what you want for yourself. It's hard to do that when you are influenced by what your parents want for you. Some teenagers respond to their parents' influence by rebelling against them, rejecting their ideas and advice. Others do the exact opposite, and try to become exactly who their parents expect them to be. I think the ideal to strive for is a healthy balance between the two. It's important to respect our parents, and consider the fact that they love us, and generally want the best for us. At the same time, it is equally important to respect ourselves, and figure out what we think is best for ourselves. Even at my age, I sometimes find it difficult to achieve this balance. When I was an adolescent, it was next to impossible.

There are times when we need to listen to our parents or guardians, because they make the rules. They are adults, and can see things in ways adolescents can't. They are often looking out for your safety with a more careful eye than you are, and make rules you may not like, but that are meant to protect you.

Sometimes it feels like our parents or guardians are being way too overprotective, and aren't giving us the freedom we want to live our lives. If you feel this way, try to talk rationally to them, and explain to them what you want and why. They are more likely to listen if you approach them in a calm, reasonable way. Most adults will not listen if you end up in a screaming match, hurling insults at them. Believe me, I've tried. If you really want to change your parents' or guardians' decision about something, the best strategy is to be calm and respectful, even if you are bubbling with rage inside.

Sometimes it's important to question things your parents or other adults tell you, and think about whether you want those ideals to guide your own life. As you grow into your own person, you might see ways in which you are different from the people who raised you. These differences can often become sources of conflict, but can also be opportunities for growth. It's completely natural to start to see these differences during adolescence. This doesn't have to be a source of stress. People can be very different from one another, and still remain close. Remember to respect people's differences, and not to judge your parents for the choices they've made, just as you don't want them to judge you for your choices.

For more about maintaining meaningful relationships with parents, flip back to Chapter Nine on dealing with stress.

## Divorce

Divorce is the breakup of a family. No matter when or how it happens, it is a stressful experience. Kids tend to think it's their fault, or that there is something they can do to get their parents back together. It's important to recognize that sometimes relationships just don't work out, or that people change over time, and it's not your fault if your parents aren't getting along. It's a really good idea to talk to a professional if your parents are going through a divorce, or if they already did, and you have some feelings about it. Talk to your parents about finding someone to help you.

## Trust

If we want our parents or guardians to trust us and respect our choices, we have to trust them too. We also have to show them that we are capable of making wise decisions for ourselves.

If you want more privileges, respect the boundaries that have been set, and show that you deserve a little more freedom. For example, if you want to be allowed to stay out later, respect the rules by coming home on time consistently. Once you've shown that you can be trusted to be home when you are expected, compromise is more likely.

If you want to be left alone about your schoolwork, be responsible about your assignments. Do work that makes you proud, and turn it in on time. If your parents or guardians consistently get calls from teachers about your irresponsibility, they are unlikely to trust you. If you need help being more on top of things at school, recognize that and ask for it. If you show your parents that you can be diligent about your work, they are more likely to see you as a more responsible person.

## Siblings

Relationships between brothers and sisters are inevitably complicated, especially when you grow up in the same house. My sister is five years younger than me, and I love her more than words can express. I would do anything for her, and I know she is always there for me too. We grew up together, and think a lot of the same things. And yet we are really different too. We dress differently, and have different friends and interests. For a long time, I think she felt that she had to be like me, or at least accomplish the same things I did, or more. Yet she has different talents, and it was important for her to grow into her own person. Once she started to do that, it was really difficult for me to accept her for who she was, because I wanted her to be more like me. I was hurt that she wanted to be different, and she was hurt because it seemed like I didn't love her for who she was. Now that we are adults, I realize that it's okay for us to be different. I love and respect her, and appreciate our differences.

## Feeling safe at home

Your house should be a place where you feel safe and comfortable. Unfortunately, many young people don't feel this way, because they are abused or neglected by their family members. Violence at home is simply not okay, and you shouldn't have to live in an environment that feels unsafe or uncomfortable to you. If you feel unsafe at home, you can get help. Talk to an adult you trust, maybe a teacher, school counselor, relative, or friend's parent. You can also call the Childhelp National Child Abuse Hotline at 1-800-4-A-CHILD (1-800-422-4453).

No matter how similar or different siblings are, it's easy to compete about almost anything, especially if you are close in age to your brother or sister. Many siblings compete about grades, or looks, or who gets more attention from their parents. I remember always thinking that my parents loved my sister more (even though I know that's not true!), and that she got her way more often than I did. I am sure she felt like I got more privileges because I was older. I got to stay up later, drive first, go out more... I am sure she felt like it wasn't fair that I got to do all those things, while she had to wait. A little competition between siblings is totally normal, but it's important not to let it get out of control.

It's also normal for siblings to argue. My sister and I definitely had our fair share of fights. But it's important to try to keep that fighting to a minimum. I have been really mean to my sister, and I knew that no matter what I said, she would still love me. If I made my friends really mad, they might abandon me. But my sister is my sister for life, no matter what I said to her. At the same time, it wasn't fair to treat her badly just because I knew she had to love me anyway. It's also not a good idea to physically fight, even though your siblings might make you angry enough to want to hit them.

Sibling relationships are intense because you know each other so well, well enough to know how to really hurt each other. I can't overstate how important it is to work as hard as you can to preserve your relationships with your siblings, no matter how challenging it might be. There is something so special about a relationship with a brother or sister, something that can't be found anywhere else. Someone who watched you grow up and stood next to you the whole way is an irreplaceable person in your life. Your relationship with your brother or sister will grow and change over time, and it is something that you can't find with anyone else. No one knows me like my sister does, and no one ever will. She's seen me go through a lifetime of emotions, and has always been there for me, to celebrate the happy times, and make the sad times easier. That is invaluable.

## Friends

I've talked a lot about friends already, and how important it is to recognize when they are hurting us too much. Some competition between friends is normal, but too much can be hurtful and destructive to relationships. It's also normal for friends to pressure each other a little, but important to recognize the difference between pressure to try new things that are good for us, and pressure to do things that might be risky or simply not what we want to do. (Chapters Four and Five get into this in more depth.)

Just as it is important to recognize when friendships are not what we want them to be, it's crucial to think about what makes a meaningful friendship, and to recognize those friends who support us, love us, and care for us in ways we can't describe. During adolescence, friends are crucial, especially as you define yourself, and start to see the ways in which you are different from your family. Friends have a big impact on what we think and how we behave, so it is very worthwhile to put some effort into developing friendships that are meaningful and special. Think about what it means to you to be a good friend. Develop a list of qualities that you look for in a friend.

## In my mind, a good friend is someone who is...

> Trustworthy. I can tell her secrets, and know she will keep them.

> Loyal. I can count on her when I need her to be there for me, and know that she won't stab me in the back if she gets the chance.

> Fun. I laugh and smile with her when we hang out.

> Interesting. I am curious to hear what is happening in her life.

> Caring. She will lend a hand when I need her to.

> Open minded. She won't judge my choices, even if they are different from hers.

> Honest. She will tell me the truth, even if it is hard for her to do that, or she knows it will be difficult for me to hear what she's saying.

> Respectful. She loves me for who I am.

Your list might be different from mine. Whatever qualities you choose, remember to seek out people who embody those qualities. Look for the kinds of people you want to be friends with, and try to surround yourself with them. Sometimes those people are not the coolest or most popular, but they are the ones who will stand by you, and take care of you when you need them. Value those people, because good friends are treasures, and are sometimes closer to you than family. Strive in all that you do to be the best friend that you can be. If you do, your friends will do the same for you.

## Elders

My mom passed away a few years ago, and since then I have realized the significance of my relationships with other women in her generation—women who are older than me, such as my aunts, older friends or teachers. These women are really important, especially when I need to feel some mom-like support. Of course, no one will ever replace my mom—and I am not looking for that—but my elder women friends are there when I need them to guide me, give a hug or just listen. Each of us can really benefit from relationships like these, even when our moms are still walking on the earth. Some subjects are just easier to discuss with someone who is not our mom, and in general, it's beneficial for us to have other women elders in our lives who inspire us and serve as examples of the women we strive to be. Life experience is really valuable and so is the opportunity to get advice from someone who is older than I am. I had the great privilege of knowing both of my grandmothers and learning from their beautiful ways of being. Now that they are no longer here with me, I enjoy relationships with other grandmothers. Find someone who is your elder—a woman who is older than you by a generation or more—who can give you love and support whenever you might need it.

## Romance

In our society, there is a ton of pressure on women to develop romantic relationships. Lots of girls think they need a significant other to be happy, and value themselves less when they are not in a relationship. Not only is this pressure unfair, but no relationship will be successful unless both people respect themselves, first and foremost. I have seen lots of friends in relationships with people who didn't treat them well. They stayed in these relationships out of fear of being alone, even though they ended up feeling worse about themselves because of the way their partners treated them.

It's easy to feel bad about yourself if you are not involved with someone romantically and your friends are. They may pressure you to find a boyfriend or girlfriend for yourself, even if you are not ready. Remember that there is no 'right' age to get involved with someone, and that it is entirely up to you to seek out these kinds of relationships or not.

That being said, being involved with someone romantically can be fun and exciting. It's inspiring to get to know someone else well, and to let them know you too. It can be hard to trust someone deeply, but when you do, this can be wonderful. Romantic relationships can be challenging too. Being close to someone might make you question things about yourself or lead you to grow or change.

No matter who you are with, open and honest communication is the most important aspect of any healthy relationship. Talk to your partner about what makes you happy, and what doesn't. If he or she is doing something you like or don't like, let him or her know. Ask your partner to share the same kind of information with you.

Having romantic feelings for someone else can be intimidating and confusing as well as exhilarating. I remember feeling really overwhelmed by my feelings for my first boyfriend. He was really special, and we cared about each other a lot, but I didn't know how to deal with those feelings. I was scared by how much my happiness was tied up in how he treated me, and found myself wanting to be independent from him. It took

## Relationship violence

"A few years ago, I had a boyfriend whom I cared for very deeply. He and I had great chemistry, and felt passionately about one another. He loved me too, and I knew it. Yet we fought all the time. I didn't like a lot of the things he said and did, and I told him. When I did this, he would get really angry and yell at me. He drank a lot, and when he was drunk, his behavior was even worse. He cursed at me, made fun of me, and generally made me feel bad about myself. He was violent a lot, though usually the violence wasn't directed at me. He'd get angry with himself and punch walls, or do other stupid stuff like that.

"His behavior scared me. At the same time, I loved him and I knew that he loved me too. I thought that if I stayed with him, we could get past the bad parts of our relationship, and focus on the good stuff. When we were getting along, it was great. We were crazy about each other. One time, he threw a glass bottle across my living room. When that happened, I knew that I had to get away from him. I realized that as much as we cared about each other, his behavior wasn't going to change. It was sad to leave him, but I can't be around him. It hurts too much." **Nina, 19**

Dating violence is a serious issue. No one should have to put up with it. Relationship violence can be verbal, physical, or emotional abuse. It's too easy to get stuck in these kinds of relationships, especially when you have strong feelings for each other. Nina loved her boyfriend, and wanted to help him through his problems. She cared about him, and didn't want to abandon him, even though his behavior was hurting her. If you are in a situation like this, get out as soon as possible. Recognize that you can't change your partner, and that he is only hurting you and himself. Talk with someone you trust about what is going on. You can call the National Domestic Violence Hotline at 1-800-799-SAFE (1-800-799-7233). Be honest. Try not to be scared. You don't have to put up with abusive treatment.

me a long time to let him into my heart, but once I did, our relationship was great. We trusted each other, and cared for one another very deeply. After a while, our feelings and our circumstances changed, and we broke up. It hurt to separate from him, but eventually I moved on and felt okay by myself again. All in all, I learned a lot from the experience of being with him, and was glad that we shared the time we did.

Romantic relationships are complicated, but like any close relationship, they can enhance your life. Be open minded about getting involved with people, but remember, first and foremost, to respect yourself, and stay in touch with your own needs.

\*\*\*

In every relationship—family, friends, partners, elders—exists the possibility to grow and get to know ourselves better. Every relationship creates the opportunity to learn and to grow closer to another person in a way that empowers me and nourishes me in the most important relationship of all—my relationship with myself.

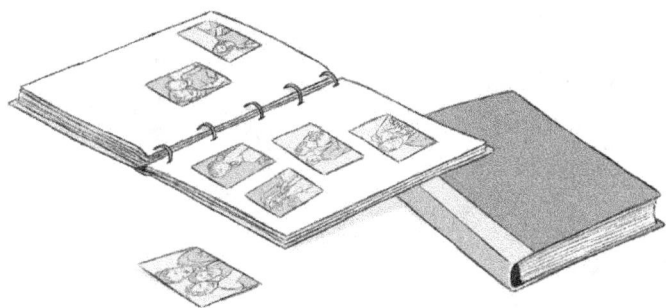

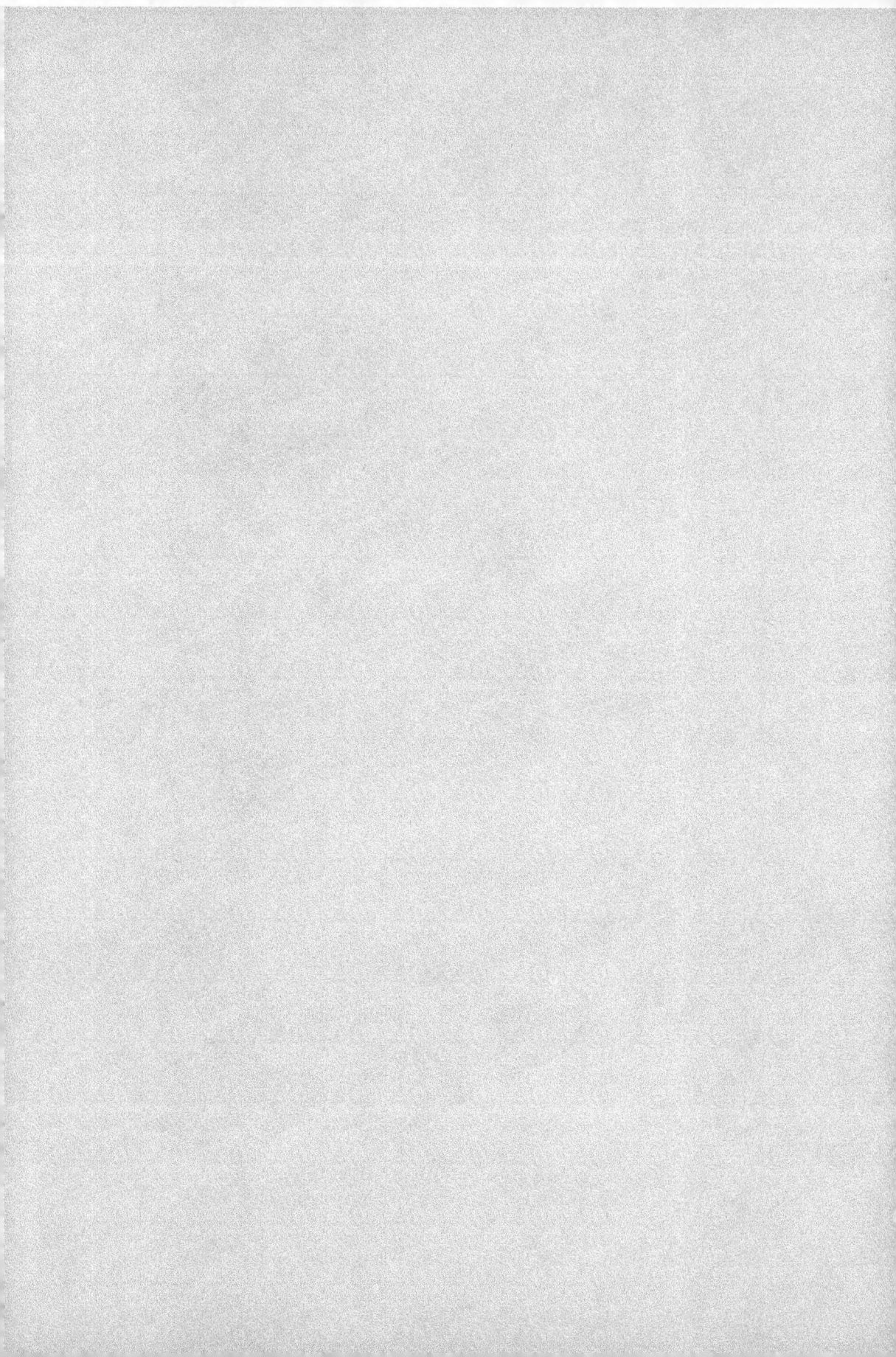

# Knowing, Respecting and Choosing Myself

It is easy for us to see how our lives are deeply impacted by the influences around us. We are aware that there are other people with whom we interact who make us think about who we are and what we believe. Our friends support us, and at the same time challenge us to resist peer pressure. Our parents ask us to define ourselves, and offer us guidelines to help us make choices. Our teachers implore us to think beyond our limits, to grapple with a world that we might not explore without their support. The media we consume—TV, magazines, movies, Internet—are like a mirror, reflecting certain aspects of the world in which we live.

In the midst of all this, the most crucial questions we can ask ourselves are those that implore us to think about who we are, and how we receive and respond to the many influences in our lives. The most important, meaningful relationship we each have is with ourselves. The way we see ourselves—the things we say when we talk to ourselves—largely determines how we will feel about everything else.

If we can feel strong and positive about who we are, then we can have strong, positive responses to the influences around us. I know it's a lot easier for me to say that than it is for you to change your attitude, but that kind of change is entirely possible, no matter how unrealistic it might seem. And the more we can learn to find happiness within ourselves, the

"Things I am proud of about me are... That I am smart That I am strong That I am capable of things people never thought I could do."

**Eliza, 13**

better off we are. If we rely on external things to make us feel good, then we are lost when those things aren't working for us. For example, if my self-image depends on how my friends see me, then I am going to feel bad about myself if my friends have a bad attitude toward me, even though their attitude might be based on absolutely nothing I've done. There's no real reason for me to be upset with myself.

"I am a girl
A female
A woman
A teenager
A daughter
And a human being."

Medina, 13

Certainly, there is no way to entirely control our happiness, and we do want to invest some measure of it into other people—friends, parents, siblings, romantic partners, teachers, grandparents, or anyone else in our lives. If we didn't invest energy in relationships, then we'd just go through the world like robots, each doing our own thing, and never caring about anyone else unless they got in our way. Life is enhanced by positive relationships, and real, meaningful ones are built upon love, attention, and care for each other and one another's feelings. But the foundation for building these positive relationships, and—more important—the foundation for living a happy, satisfying life in general is to nourish a positive relationship with yourself.

I know that I can always rely on myself. I will never let myself down, and I can be sure that looking inside will make me happy, because I am proud of the person I am. The same is true for you.

There are a million things out there giving us reasons not to be proud of ourselves. There are also tons of reasons for us to feel stressed out. But if we are strong inside, we don't have to let those things affect the way we see ourselves, at least not too much. We can remember that we are confident, capable women who have the power to see the world in the way we want to see it, not the way other people want us to see it.

"I am proud to be a girl who plays sports, because boys say girls can't, but we can! Women give birth and boys don't know what it feels like (neither do I), but I might, and that's cool!" Emma, 13

"I am proud of my femininity, and what choices girls have. I feel girls all have so many connections to one another because we all have to go through more pain than men (like pregnancy), making us stronger in our hearts." Lizzie, 13

I think that we've suffered from a great confusion over the past two generations or so, one that tells us women that in order to be equal to men, we need to be the same. This is how women began wearing clothes that look the same as men's clothing (suits, for example) and began to do things that men do. I embrace the fact that I am a woman, and I celebrate my femininity. I celebrate those unique qualities that make me a woman. And I know that from that place, I am equal to the men around me. Being equal does not mean being the same. It means equally valuing both men and women, as well as equally valuing men's work and women's work. In some traditions, women are considered more than equal, on a spiritually higher level, in large part because of our ability to grow life and give birth. This is a great miracle that I celebrate every day.

"I am someone who other people have fought for the rights of for many years. You better respect me, not just my ass. Look at my face, dummy, when you are talking to me. I am powerful and strong, and will do more in my lifetime than you could ever hope to do. I am me." Medina, 13

"Confidence is in every woman. It's waiting for the perfect time when it can show itself. It grows during your life. It's always there, whether you know it or not." Benazir, 13

"I am glad to be a woman, because then I don't have to go to an all-boys school. I can paint my nails and wear makeup as a normal thing in life. I can be pretty. I don't have to be expected to be all muscles. And mainly, I can wear cool clothes." Natalie, 13

"'You make me feel like a natural woman.' That isn't true. I am my own woman, and I am proud to say, I make myself feel like a natural woman. The word girl might be delivered as an insult, but in reality, GIRL is my life, GIRL is beautiful, GIRL is power. GIRL and WOMAN are strength and beauty. I see no insult." Shabnam, 13

The reason I know you are capable of seeing the world in this way is because I learned to see it like this from girls just like you. My students have shown me how they have found ways to close their eyes to the negative influences, and see the good in the world. They've modeled confidence, strength, and empowerment; all I've done is remind them who they are and reflect to them when they are showing those characteristics. When I finished teaching my first class, I wrote a letter to my students telling them all the amazing things I had learned from them, and thanking them for teaching me these incredible lessons. Here it is for you to read:

"On the first day of this class, I walked into a room full of beautiful, bright-eyed young women. I wish you could have seen your own faces on that day—I thought your eyes were going to pop out of your heads. You were all eager to share your own experiences, and hear those of others. I was extremely excited, but a little nervous, as I looked into your shining faces. I was eager to talk to you and hear what you had to say, but also scared that you thought I had all the answers. In truth, I had little clue what the class would be about when we started on that day. I mean, I had planned plenty, and had a general idea what we were going to do, but I had a feeling that if I just let you talk, the class would take on a life of its own.

"I never could have guessed how much I was going to learn from you, and how much your words and stories were going to affect me. I never would have thought that the way I look at the world was going to be entirely changed by hearing about your experiences. I now see things in terms of how they affect you, in terms of how media images and people's words can make or break the way you feel that day, that week, or that year. I also never would have realized how powerful it can be to talk about those things with other women. Hearing you share your thoughts with one another reminded me how important it is to talk about my own experiences with other people who understand them.

"I leave this experience proud of myself for having inspired you to be proud, smart, beautiful, and interesting women. I leave this experience even prouder of you for being those women. It is much easier for me to be a confident, self-assured woman than it is for you—I have had many more years to become comfortable with myself. According to all the books, you should be at the highest point of your insecurity, but you defy all expectations, are proud to be who you are, and are not likely to let stereotypes stand in your way. I doubt that anyone will ever stop you from doing something you want to do because you are female, although people might try. In fact, I think that if anyone were to try, you would be even more motivated to succeed and prove them wrong. You go girls!

"Thank you for helping me to become the teacher and the person that I am. Thank you for influencing me to help other young women; I plan to work with other girls as I continue my journey, and to develop the curriculum for this class to share with other teachers. Thank you, most of all, for being you. Words cannot describe how truly incredible you are. Know that, and carry it with you forever. Much love."

Know that you teach people every day. Your words and actions impact those around you. Use your power to impact others for good, in order to help make the world a better place. The most basic thing you can do to influence others positively is to think positive thoughts about yourself every day. Even if it sounds cheesy, look in the mirror, smile at yourself, and be proud of the beautiful woman you are. Your attitude will affect others.

Remember that the language we use has a big impact. The way we talk about ourselves has an effect on the way we see ourselves. Use language that is empowering, particularly when talking about something you want to change. Saying "I can do better," is encouraging, while saying "I am terrible at that," will just bring me down. I can choose to use my words to make me stronger, and to emphasize my capabilities.

Listen to yourself. By listening to your inner voice, you can make decisions about what is best for you in any given situation. Make smart choices that you will be proud of when you reflect on them. When you make bad choices, remember them and learn, so you won't make them again.

Remind yourself all the time that you are smart and capable. You accomplish so many things that you might never have thought you could do. When you doubt your abilities to achieve, challenge yourself by setting a goal you know you can realize, but only if you put in some real effort. Maybe your goal will be to run a set distance, sew your own skirt, write a poem, teach someone something, plant a garden, or paint a portrait. Whatever it is, do the best you can to realize it. Because you know that you can, you will learn as you try, and will feel good about yourself when you've done what you set out to do.

Don't forget how important you are to the people around you. There are lots of people out there, including yourself, who rely on you to be their support, to help them when they are down, and smile with them when they are happy.

Talk to people you care for and trust about the things I've asked you to think about in this book. I hope the things I say will be the beginning of a longer discussion with your friends, parents, teachers, and, most of all, with yourself. I've asked you about things that might never be fully resolved for you, things you might question yourself about for years to come. There are many topics I've brought up that I think about all the time. That's why I wrote this book—to help you think about these topics by exposing my own ideas as food for thought. There are lots of things in this world that make me wonder. The best way I know how to deal with them is to share my questions with others. Together we can support each other, and talk about our ideas for manifesting change.

Being a teenager isn't easy. But that doesn't mean that you can't go through this time gracefully, learning about yourself and about the world along the way. Sure, there will be challenges, times when you wonder if things will be okay. When those times come, look inside yourself, and know that you are a beautiful, amazing, brilliant young woman who can do whatever she sets her mind to. If you know that about yourself, you can achieve anything. Smile and keep that joy with you always.

**Be proud of who you are.**

👁 Naomi

# CHAPTER NOTES

## Chapter One

1.    Friedman, Sandra Susan. When Girls Feel Fat: *Helping Girls Through Adolescence*. Buffalo, NY: Firefly Books, 2000.

2.    Parry, Vivienne. "It's Not Just the Hormones..." *The Guardian*, March 2, 2005. www.guardian.co.uk

3.    Drill, Esther, Heather McDonald, and Rebecca Odes. *Deal With It! A Whole New Approach to Your Body*, Brain and Life as a gURL. New York: Gallery Books, 1999.

4.    Wiseman, Rosalind. *Queen Bees and Wannabes: Helping Your Daughter Survive Cliques, Gossip, Boyfriends, and Other Realities of Adolescence*. New York: Crown, 2002.

## Chapter Two

    *From Girl to Woman—What Girls Should Know about Growing Up*. South Deerfield, MA: Channing L. Bete Co., Inc., 1997.

1.    "Plastic Surgery Statistics Report." American Society of Plastic Surgeons, Clearinghouse of Plastic Surgery Procedural Statistics. www.plasticsurgery.org

2.    "PERFECT ILLUSIONS: Eating Disorders and the Family." www.pbs.org

3.    Kilbourne, Jean. "Killing Us Softly 4"—Trailer www.jeankilbourne.com

4.    "The Merchants of Cool," PBS, February 2001. www.pbs.org

## Chapter Three

1.    Kaiser Permanente brochure, The Permanente Medical Group, 2001.

2.    "The Diet Industry: A Big Fat Lie." www.businessweek.com

3.    "Educate Yourself, "About-Face.org. www.about-face.org.

4.    Kaiser Permanente brochure

5.    "Statistics on Eating Disorders: Anorexia, Bulimia and Binge Eating." www.eatingdisorderhope.com

## Chapter Six

1-3.    Sales, Nancy Jo. *American Girls: Social Media and the Secret Lives of Teenagers*. New York, NY: Knopf, 2016.

4.    Twenge, Jean M. "Have Smartphones Destroyed a Generation?" *The Atlantic*. September 2017. www.theatlantic.com

5.    "Social Media, Social Life: How Teens View their Digital Lives." *Common Sense Media*. 26 June 2012. www.commonsensemedia.org

    Tsukuyama, Hayley. "Teens Spend Nearly Nine Hours Every Day Consuming Media." *The Washington Post*. 3 November 2015. www.washingtonpost.com

    Young, Katie. "Social Media Captures Over 30% of Online Time." Global Web Index. 11 September 2017. blog.globalwebindex.net

**6-7.** Lenhart, Amanda. "Teens, Social Media and Technology Overview 2015." Pew Research Center. 9 April 2015. www.pewInternet.org

**8.** Stern, Robin. 25 December 2017. Personal Interview.

**9.** Fulghum Bruce, Debra. "Teen Internet Safety Tips." WebMD. teens.webmd.com

**10.** Marsh, Sarah. "Girls suffer under pressure of 'online perfection,' poll finds." *The Guardian.* 23 August 2017 www.theguardian.com

**11.** Schurgin O'Keefe, Gwenn and Kathleen Clarke-Pearson. "The Impact of Social Media on Children, Adolescents and Families." *Pediatrics.* April 2011, Volume 127/Issue 4. pediatrics.aappublications.org

**12.** Mabe, Analise G., K. Jean Forney and Pamela K. Keel. "Do You Like My Photo? Facebook Use Maintains Eating Disorder Risk." *International Journal of Eating Disorders.* January 2014, Volume 47, Issue 5. onlinelibrary.wiley.com

**13-16.** Twenge, Jean M. "Have Smartphones Destroyed a Generation?"

**17.** Sales, Nancy Jo. *American Girls: Social Media and the Secret Lives of Teenagers.*

**18.** Yandel, Jeannie. "'Her Eyes are Bigger than Her Waist' Peggy Orenstein on Selling Girls on the Idea of Being Hot." *The Record,* KUOW. 15 June 2016. kuow.org

**19-20.** Hill, Anna and Lemaja Denman. "Adolescent Self-Esteem and Instagram: An Examination of Posting Behaviors." Concordia University-St. Paul. docplayer.net

**21-22.** Sales, Nancy Jo. "You inspire me to be hot and famous: How Kim Kardashian became a teen idol." *The Guardian.* 25 February 2016. www.theguardian.com

**23.** Sales, Nancy Jo. *American Girls: Social Media and the Secret Lives of Teenagers.*

**24-25.** Stern, Robin. 25 December 2017. Personal Interview.

## Chapter Seven

**1.** Orenstein, Peggy. "When Did Porn Become Sex Ed?" *NY Times*, 19 March 2016. www.nytimes.com

**2.** Sellegren, Katherine. "Pornography 'desensitizing young people.'" *BBC*, 15 June 2016. www.bbc.com

**3.** Lauffer-Zeevi, Tohar. 13 December 2018. Personal interview.

**4.** *Deal With It!* (See Chapter One, Note 3)

## Chapter Eight

**1.** *Deal With It!* (See Chapter One, Note 3)

## Chapter Nine

**1-2.** Depression information from Kaiser Permanente

## Work with Naomi

The foundation of the work I do is my prayer
that every young woman will know
in the deepest reaches of her heart
that she is not alone
that she is loved
that she deserves to be honored and celebrated
that her voice must be heard
that her words are important.

I dedicate my work to this goal,
to manifest a world
in which every girl, every woman values herself
in which every boy, every man honors himself
and the women in his life.

To achieve this end, I travel throughout the world offering workshops,
keynote presentations and consulting/program development for
schools and organizations.

For more information, visit **www.naomikatz.com**.

**Her Wisdom**
**Cultivating the uniqueness of women's leadership**

The central questions that guide my work are: How do we educate girls as they become women? What initiation do we want to offer them?

In the year following the publication of the first edition of *Beautiful*, I traveled extensively, working together with many girls and their mentors and observing the particular ways in which women and girls are learning to embody themselves. In a wide variety of contexts, all over the world, I saw that women and girls are deeply impacted by the message that being equal means being the same, that being a successful woman—whatever that might mean to each of us—means adopting leadership qualities that are masculine in nature.

In light of this observation, I established Her Wisdom, a non-profit organization dedicated to cultivating the uniqueness and authenticity of women's leadership. For more information about Her Wisdom, visit **www.herwisdom.org**.

Together, we are redefining culture for women and girls.

www.ingramcontent.com/pod-product-compliance
Lightning Source LLC
Chambersburg PA
CBHW080643270326
41928CB00017B/3175